TWAYNE'S WORLD AUTHORS SERIES
A Survey of the World's Literature

VENEZUELA

Luis Davila, Indiana University

EDITOR

Mariano Picón Salas

TWAS 545

MARIANO PICÓN SALAS

By THOMAS D. MORIN
University of Rhode Island

TWAYNE PUBLISHERS

A DIVISION OF G. K. HALL & CO., BOSTON

PQ
8549
.P5
278

Published in 1979 by Twayne Publishers,
A Division of G. K. Hall & Co.
All Rights Reserved

Printed on permanent/durable acid-free paper and bound
in the United States of America

First Printing

Frontispiece photograph of Mariano Picón Salas.

Library of Congress Cataloging in Publication Data

Morin, Thomas D   1938–
Mariano Picón Salas.

(Twayne's world authors series ; TWAS 545: Venezuela)
Bibliography: p. 140–52
Includes index.
1. Picón Salas, Mariano, 1901–1965—Criticism and interpretation.
PQ8549.P5Z78   864   78–27053

ISBN 0–8057–6388–0

To M. and Tommy

Contents

About the Author

Preface

Acknowledgments

Chronology

1. Historical Background   17

2. Mariano Picón Salas: Essayist   34

3. Toward a Quest for Identity   52

4. *Errancia:* A Spiritual Becoming and
   an Intellectual Awakening   62

5. An Intellectual Voyage   73

6. Europe and America   100

7. A Search for Paradise Lost   118

8. Conclusion   127

Notes and References   131

Selected Bibliography   140

Index   153

About the Author

Thomas D. Morin was born in Hoboken, New Jersey, in 1938. He graduated from Rutgers University in 1960 with a B.A. in Romance Languages. Italian was his major area of concentration and Spanish his minor. Upon graduation he entered into military service and served for two years in the U.S. Army in the Canal Zone. In 1963 he began teaching English and Spanish at the U.S. Air Force School for Latin America. At the same time he was employed as an English instructor for the bicultural institute Instituto Panameño Norteamericano in Panama City, Panama. He returned to the U.S. in 1965 and began graduate studies at Columbia University receiving a National Defense Fellowship for Languages. In 1968 he received his Masters in Spanish. He taught at St. Francis College. He received his Ph.D. from Columbia University in 1975. He also taught at City College of New York, Hunter College, Borough of Manhattan Community College, New York Community College, Columbia University, and since 1975 he has taught at the University of Rhode Island, where he is an Assistant Professor and Chairman of the Latin American Studies Program. In 1977 he published a joint article along with Professor Robert Weisbord, Professor of History, at the University of Rhode Island, entitled "The Caribbean Refuge." This article was the result of a research project to the Dominican Republic in 1976. His present interests include the Latin American essay and Latin American Area Studies.

Preface

Peregrination has long been established as a literary theme in Western literature. The central theme of Homer's *Odyssey*, for example, is one of a journey within the world of Greek mythology. Similarly, in Spanish literature, the trajectory of *El Cid* is a journey of exile and struggle on the part of Ruy Díaz De Vivar to win back his honor. In *Don Quixote*, the theme of peregrination juxtaposes the physical aspect of voyaging along with a more subtle intellectual peregrination of the mind of the knight errant Dox Quixote.

Peregrination, seen from a literary perspective, has become an essential ingredient in the development of idealism as a spiritual force in the world. Peregrination, either in the physical world or in the spiritual, leads the traveler toward something better, a new utopia. Conversely, a journey or voyage may also presuppose a desire to purge the individual spirit or society of what is considered outdated or shopworn.

One of the objectives of this study is to demonstrate the nature of Picón Salas' peregrination as a physical and intellectual, or spiritual journey, leading toward self-identity and the search for utopia. I also wish to establish the essayist's peregrination as a search for cultural authenticity, which possesses the dual elements of alienation and reintegration. Through the concept of reintegration I intend to show the trajectory of peregrination as a circular design. In *Don Quixote*, the fearless knight errant is constantly returning to the house and library of Don Quijano el Bueno in order to regain his spiritual strength and rebuild his illusions. In Picón Salas, as we shall see, the journey away from and back to Venezuela is a voyage to the center of personal existence.

In Latin America, the fictional voyage in search of utopia is directly related to the physical reality of the Conquest itself. Bernal Díaz del Castillo, in his chronicles of the sixteenth century, demonstrated how the hope of finding the utopia mentioned in the Spanish chivalric novels existed as a realistic goal in the minds of the Spanish conquerors. The twentieth-century Latin American essay is an attempt to recreate the ideals of the Spanish conquerors, who saw in the American continent a new and more promising world. In my study, I wish to demonstrate the union between the spiritual goals of the individual and the historical reality in which he lives, and how through this combination of elements Picón Salas discovers his personal identity and the cultural identity of the American continent.

One of the more difficult problems encountered in preparing this study was the limited accessibility to Picón Salas' works. The reasons for this are several. In the first place, the author's books, excepting one or two, did not have a very large distribution. Most of them are now out of print. Second, Picón Salas wrote his essays while sojourning throughout the world and had them published in numerous newspapers and periodicals. No one has succeeded in collecting all of the essays in book form. In a special section of the bibliography I have provided a list of the essays that Picón Salas published in *El Nacional*, a leading newspaper of Venezuela, wherein the essayist directed a Sunday supplement entitled "Papel literario" ("Literary Notes").

The study is divided into eight chapters. Chapter 1 presents the historical background which situates the writer in the Latin American milieu. The brief historical background of the political developments in Venezuela and in Latin America, in general, is necessary for understanding the essays included in this study. Chapter 2 is an examination of the author's interpretation of the essay as a literary genre and the particular relationship between Picón Salas and his work. Chapter 3 examines the initial stages in the author's intellectual development. It should be considered a prelude to all that follows. Chapter 4 examines the concept of peregrination, or *errancia*, as a physical and intellectual movement away from the center of personal existence. Chapter 5 presents the author's physical and intellectual voyage away from Venezuela and into the larger cultural reality of Latin America; it also establishes the circular nature of peregrination as a going-out-from and returning-to the center of existence. Chapter 6 deals with Picón Salas' observations on Europe and America and presents the author's views on the cultural milieu in

Venezuela and his effort to establish a personal identity with the spirit of his nation. Chapter 7 is an analysis of Picón Salas' autobiographical *Viaje al amanecer*, situated in the Venezuelan province of Mérida and his attempt to redefine, in light of his travels throughout the world, the meaning of his past life. In the Conclusion, I summarize the author's views and demonstrate his contributions to the world of Latin American thought.

This study does not examine all the author's works. I have chosen only those books and essays which seem to demonstrate best the essential theme of peregrination and the author's use of the essay as a literary genre. Picón's two novels, *Pedro Claver, santo de los esclavos* (*Pedro Claver, the Saint of the Slaves*), and *Los tratos de la noche* (*Nights Deals*), have not been treated at length. The latter is only mentioned in passing. Nor have I treated to any great degree those works which primarily deal with historical subjects such as in *Los días de Cipriano Castro* (*The Days of Cipriano Castro*), and *Literatura Venezolana* (*Venezuelan Literature*), *Hispanoamérica, posición crítica* (*Hispanic America, A Critical Position*), and *De la conquista a la Independencia, tres siglos de historia cultural* (*From the Conquest to Independence: Three Centuries of Cultural History*).

I am responsible for the translations from Picón's essays which appear in the body of this text. At times I have taken the liberty, for benefit of those readers who have little knowledge about the author and his country, to insert in these translations phrases which clarify the cultural and historical meaning conveyed in the original text.

T. D. MORIN

Kingston, Rhode Island

Acknowledgments

The research for this study was carried on in the United States, Mexico, and Venezuela. I would like to offer my gratitude to those who have inspired me to complete this work: Professor Andres Iduarte, essayist and professor at Columbia University from 1939 to 1975; Professors Armand Chartier and Robert Monteiga, colleagues and friends at the University of Rhode Island; and to Professor Billy Bussell Thompson of Columbia University.

In Venezuela I interviewed the first wife of Picón Salas, Isabel Cento, and Delia Isabel, the only daughter of the essayist. I would also like to express my appreciation for their comments. Appreciation is also extended to Luis Beltrán Guerrero for his hospitality and to Marta Mosquera and Rafael Piñeda. To Beatriz Otañez de Picón Salas, the essayist's second wife, goes my appreciation for permitting me entry to the den and library of the author.

The section of the bibliography listing the essays published in *El Nacional* would have been impossible without the assistance of Arturo Uslar Pietri.

I would also like to express my gratitude to Ms. Vivian Wohl for her patience and professionalism in preparing the original manuscript.

Finally, my fondest affection and appreciation to Miryam and Thomas, my son, who had to endure many frustrating moments during the preparation of this text. It is to them and to my parents, Anthony and Ann Morin, that I dedicate this work.

Chronology

1901 Mariano Picón Salas born January 26, in Mérida, Venezuela.

1917 First published essay, *Las nuevas corrientes del arte,* presented on October 28, to the University of Los Andes.

1918 Publication of the brief essay *En las puertas de un mundo nuevo (Ensayo de crítica social).*

1920 University studies in Caracas. Publishes first book, *Buscando el camino.*

1923 Leaves Caracas for Chile due to oppression of Venezuelan dictator, Juan Vicente Gómez. Arrives in Santiago where he continues his university studies. Becomes superintendent of education. Assists in founding the Faculty of Philosophy and Letters.

1927 *Mundo imaginario; Los recuerdos impresionistas, La vida de hombre, Historia de un amigo, Tema de amor.*

1928– Professor of philosophy and letters at the Univer-
1936 sity of Chile.

1929 With Salvador Reyes and Hernán del Solar founds the literary review *Letras.*

1930– Participates in the founding of the literary group,
1934 *Indice.*

1931 *Hispanoamérica, posición crítica* and *Odisea de tierra firme.*

1934 *Problemas y métodos de la historia del arte: Dos conferencias didácticas;* and *Registro de huéspedes.*

1935 *Intuición de Chile y otros ensayos en busca de una conciencia histórica.*

1936 Returns to Venezuela after the death of the dictator to become superintendent of the Ministry of Education.

1936–1937	Chargé d'affaires in Prague.
1937	*Preguntas a Europa: Viajes y ensayos.*
1938–1940	Director of Culture and Fine Arts in the Ministry of Education.
1940	*1941. Cinco discursos sobre el pasado y presente de la nación venezolana; Un viaje y seis retratos, Formación y proceso de la literatura venezolana.*
1942–1944	Visiting professor at Columbia University, Middlebury College, Smith College, and the University of California at Berkeley.
1943	*Viaje al amanecer.*
1944	*De la conquista a la independencia; Tres siglos de historia cultural de hispanoamericana.*
1946	*Miranda.*
1946–1947	Dean and founder of the faculty of Philosophy and Letters of the Universidad Central de Venezuela.
1947	*Europa-América.*
1947–1948	Venezuelan ambassador in Colombia.
1949	*Comprensión de Venezuela.*
1949	Visiting professor at the University of Puerto Rico in San Juan.
1950	*Pedro Claver, el santo de los esclavos.*
1951	Visiting professor at the University of California at Los Angeles.
1951–1958	Professor in the Faculty of Humanities and Education at the Universidad Central in Venezuela.
1952	*Dependencia e independencia en la historia hispanoamericana.*
1953	*Los días de Cipriano Castro; Simón Rodríguez, Suramérica: período colonial.*
1954	Receives the National Prize for Literature in Venezuela.
1955	*Los tratos de la noche* and *Crisis, cambio y tradición.*
1958	*Las nieves de antaño: Pequeña añoranza de Mérida.* Venezuelan embassador to Brazil.
1959	*Despedida do Brasil, Regreso de tres mundos, Un hombre en su generación.*

Chronology

1959–1962	Venezuelan delegate to UNESCO in Paris.
1962	*Los malos salvajes* and *Civilización y política contemporáneas*. Venezuelan embassador to Mexico.
1963	Secretary general in Venezuelan cabinet. *Hora y deshora; temas humanísticos, nombres y figuras, viajes y lugares*.
1964	President of the National Institute of Culture and Fine Arts, Caracas.
1965	January 1, dies at a New Year's Eve party in Caracas.

CHAPTER 1

Historical Background

I General

IN the nineteenth century the Spanish American countries received their political and economic independence from Spain. Simón Bolívar, the Venezuelan Liberator, conceived the idea of Pan-Americanism in the hope of complementing political independence with the creation of a spiritual and cultural ideal capable of uniting the land masses of Central and South America into one homogeneous whole. Bolívar knew that independence had to develop as a state of consciousness within the minds of the inhabitants of the hemisphere; there had to exist an awareness of the spiritual integrity of the land and its political institutions. However, after the Wars for Independence, the Bolivarian dream of Spanish American unity shattered, with the fragmentation of the old colonial empire, into many politically independent regions and sub-regions ruled by local dictators, or *caudillos*. Bolívar's effort to create even a modified version of Pan-American unity in the state of Gran Colombia soon disintegrated, and Bolívar, at the end of his life, resigned himself to the thought of having plowed in the ocean.

After Independence eighteen autonomous countries were formed. The years that followed the Wars of Independence were characterized by civil discord and strife. Venezuela suffered an inordinate amount due to the violence of a fratricidal struggle for power. The political issues that predominated toward the middle of the nineteenth century and which seemed to spark the Wars of Federation were the issues of liberalism and federalism versus conservatism and centralization. The Wars of Federation were fought between those who sought to maintain regional control of

17

the country as the basis for the political system and those more conservative elements who advocated a strong central government based in Caracas.[1] By the time civil order was restored under the leadership of Antonio Guzmán Blanco in 1870, the violence had nearly halved the male population of the country. Laureano Vallenilla Lanz, a Venezuelan historian and sociologist, attempted to show in *Disgregación e integración* (*Separation and Integration*) that the problem of political and social disunity represented in the Wars of Federation was the result of the particular organic structure of Venezuelan society.[2] Carlos Irazábal has interpreted the cause of national disunity and civil war in Venezuela as being the result of an essential contradiction between the prevailing social and economic reality and the political ideals of Venezuela's leaders beginning with Bolívar. For Irazábal, the ideal of a republican form of government could not develop in the nineteenth century because of the economic situation that maintained the subjugation of the many by the few.[3]

The political phenomenon that dominated the nineteenth century was *caudillismo,* a form of dictatorial rule peculiar to Spanish America. George S. Wise has attempted to define this form of dictatorship as something between the old-world concept of dynasty and the twentieth-century version of the ideological ruler.[4] Wise chose as a prototype for his study of *caudillismo* the Venezuelan dictator Antonio Guzmán Blanco, who ruled between 1870 and 1889. As indicated by Wise, *caudillismo* developed not as an ideology but, ironically, from the very democratic aspirations that sought to establish in Spanish America a more modern world. The rule of the caudillo began with regional control of different portions of the country. His rule was ruthless, and he personally controlled all governmental power and justice. Moreover, his ability to control the people was based on the lack of education of the majority of the population and the poverty that characterized the economic situation of the country. Through the acquistion of great power the caudillo became the ruler of the entire country. An aura of mystery usually developed around the figure of the caudillo; the people attributed his power and his cunning to natural and, sometimes, supernatural forces. In Latin America some of the more important caudillos were José Gaspar Rodríguez de Francia in Paraguay, Juan Manuel Rosas in Argentina, Gabriel García Moreno in Ecuador, and Porfirio Díaz in Mexico. In Venezuela the list of caudillos begins with José Antonio Páez. He was followed by José Tadeo Monagas, Juan Crisóstomo Falcón, Antonio Guzmán Blanco, Joaquín Crespo, Cipriano Castro, and Juan Vicente Gómez. For the most part, *caudillismo* was replaced at the turn of the century by military dictatorships. *Caudillismo* lasted longer in Venezuela than in any other country in Latin America. This situation did not ease till the death of Juan Vicente Gómez in 1936.

During the latter part of the nineteenth century the spirit of scientific positivism strongly effected the intellectual life of Latin America. It was thought that, by the introduction of the scientific method and technology, the social, political, and economic ills of the country could be cured. Two of the Latin American caudillos who adopted a positivist policy in governing the land were Porfirio Díaz in Mexico and Antonio Guzmán Blanco in Venezuela. Guzmán Blanco established the order necessary to dissipate the violence that preceded his rule. Modern technology was introduced to Venezuela; Caracas began to change from a traditional and colonial city to a modern city equipped with boulevards and public buildings. Nevertheless, Guzmán Blanco's attitude toward the rural masses remained paternalistic and typical of the caudillos who preceded his rule.[5]

The social and political problems in Latin America during the latter part of the nineteenth century were further complicated by the United States' attempt to achieve economic and political hegemony over the hemisphere. In 1898 the United States went to war with Spain, defeated that nation, and gained possession of the last vestiges of Spanish colonial rule: Cuba and Puerto Rico. During the first decade of the twentieth century the United States acquired control of the Panama Canal and landed United States Marines on the Yucatán Peninsula and in Nicaragua. By 1918 the United States was becoming, in Venezuela, the most important investor in oil production.[6]

For Latin American intellectuals, at the turn of the century, it became patently clear that the struggle for independence had not been resolved in the nineteenth century. The hemisphere was suffering from the bankrupt policies of caudillo

regimes and the continued economic disparity between the
haves and have-nots. It was feared that United States economic
influence in the southern portion of the continent would
jeopardize the political independence Latin America had
achieved. In much of the literature of the time, as in the work of
José Enrique Rodó, the United States became identified as the
Colossus of the North.[7] It was feared that the cultural heritage
of Latin America was being undermined by the introduction of a
materialism imported from the United States, a system diametrically opposed to the spiritualism of Latin America. To counter
the weight of United States cultural and economic influence, the
Latin American intellectual began to discover the spiritual essence
of national and continental identity. In the works of essayists
like Pedro Henríquez Ureña, José Carlos Mariátegui, Mariano
Picón Salas, Alfonso Reyes, José Enrique Rodó, José Vasconcelos,
and others, there was an attempt to redefine the cultural identity
and unity of Spanish America as first perceived in the idealism
of Simón Bolívar.[8] Inherent in the work of these essayists was
the concept of an existing substratum of Spanish American unity
which, if revealed, would convert chaos into political and social
harmony and order.[9] Influenced, in part, by José Ortega y
Gasset, the twentieth-century essayists came to understand
that it was impossible for man to escape his environment. Furthermore, the events in Europe during the second decade of
the century stifled attempts, at the turn of the century, to look
abroad for solutions to Latin America's cultural and political
dilemma.[10] Yet it was impossible for the essayists mentioned above
to ignore the traditions of Western civilization. In Latin America
the Spanish cultural influence predominated over that of indigenous cultures. It was the essayists' task, therefore, to discover
in the universality of Western tradition the particular expression
of that tradition in Latin America; and they accordingly attempted to dissolve the social and political polarization that
developed in the nineteenth century.

II   *Literature and Culture*

Latin American essayists, beginning with Domingo Faustino
Sarmiento, have attempted to identify continental culture and
its place in the Western cultural tradition from the vantage
point of their particular experience. The trajectory of their

work, for the most part, moves from the specific to the general, or from the particular circumstance to the more universal. For Sarmiento, in the nineteenth century, the particular circumstance of his essays is Argentina. In *Facundo o Civilización y barbarie* (*Facundo or Civilization and Barbarism*), Sarmiento offers a picture of the struggle in the hemisphere to establish a civilized society; in *Viajes por Europa, Africa y América* (*Trips through Europe, Africa and America*), he contemplates other civilizations and seeks to establish a connection between these cultures and Spanish American culture. José Carlos Mariátegui presents in his study of the Peruvian reality entitled *Siete ensayos en busca de la realidad peruana* (*Seven Essays in Search of Peruvian Reality*) a microcosm of the socioeconomic conditions that prevailed in Spanish America as a whole. For José Vasconcelos, the center of his intellectual and literary existence is México. Vasconcelos attempts to demonstrate the potential of creole culture in becoming the new utopia of the world. Alfonso Reyes, another Mexican humanist, seeks to define the cultural continuity that situated Latin America within the cultural history of Western civilization. In José Enrique Rodó's essays, the conception of Latin American reality is more abstract. Rodó is concerned with the spiritual values of the Spanish American cultural heritage. In the work of Mariano Picón Salas, the movement from the particular to the universal begins with the individual, or artist, who proceeds to discover the identity of the Venezuelan circumstance. Venezuelan reality itself becomes another element of particularity as the author then seeks to define the relationship between country and continent. In turn, the continent of America is represented as a particular form of cultural entity in the tradition of Western civilization.

Venezuela, for Picón Salas, is the fundamental reality, or particular form of existence, through which the individual discovers his personal identity, both as a Venezuelan and as a Spanish American. Between the specific reality and the more general one there exists a social, emotional, and intellectual relationship. The external, or larger reality, of the land is transformed into a kind of spiritual geography that structures the author's identity as an individual. The interaction between the individual and the environment, which Picón Salas accepts as inevitable, imposes on the artist a two-fold obligation: to comprehend the total dimension of the country's reality; and, to project that reality meaningfully in the pursuit of a better future. Picón Salas states that his literary mission is to unite the heterogeneous elements of the nation into a cultural unity and spiritual concept of Venezuelan nationhood: "it is our professional obligation to act and think in a nation engaged in a tortuous and contradictory process of growth, and to become involved in uniting within our culture the heterogeneous elements that still make up our nation." [11] The heterogeneous elements alluded to in the above quotation concern the disparities between political reality and ideals, between the effects of culture and civilization and those of the Venezuelan wilderness, and finally between the needs of the individual and the conditions imposed by society.

More than many of the essayists previously mentioned, Mariano Picón Salas united the search for self-identity with a broader search for national identity. In Picón Salas' work a preoccupation with the individual as the nucleus of society is joined to the view that the individual can only bring to fruition his full potential working in concert with other members of the society. By extension, Venezuela can only develop its talents within the cultural history of Latin America. That is to say, Venezuela, as a particular country within the continent, can and must discover its real identity as a member of the Spanish American community of nations. The latter, in turn, as it develops an awareness of the cultural factors of creole society, can only maintain the integrity of its cultural heritage by recognizing the common legacy of colonial history.

The search for a way to integrate the particular with the universal is evident in the physical and intellectual peregrination, or *errancia*, as Picón Salas stated, which is the subject of this study. In order to discover the interrelationship between the individual and the larger society, and between the particularity of Venezuelan circumstance and the circumstances of life in Spanish America, Picón Salas established a pattern of constant exploration that led him from the province of Mérida, to Caracas, and later to Chile, where he was to remain for thirteen years. The spiritual effect of the physical voyage was to transform the provincialism of his youth into a more universal spirit of cosmopolitanism. In 1937 Picón Salas extended the trajectory of his journey to the European

continent where he served, for a time, as chargé d'affaires
for the Venezuelan government in Prague. The result of that
trip was a series of essays entitled *Europa-América,
preguntas a la esfinge de la cultura (Europe-America,
Questions Put to the Sphinx of Culture)*, in which the author
sought to comprehend the relationship between the established
cultures of Europe and the cultural identity of America still
in the process of forming. In 1942, 1943, and 1950, Picón
Salas accepted teaching positions in the United States at
Middlebury College and Columbia University. He also served
as ambassador to Columbia, Mexico, and Brazil, and as
Venezuelan representative to the Executive Council of UNESCO
in Paris. These experiences assisted in the intellectual development of the essayist that led him from concerns for
Venezuelan identity to themes involving the moral and intellectual development of modern Western culture. In *Hora y
deshora (Time and Inopportune Time)*, Picón Salas expressed
the need to extend his literary mission as a commentator on
the general social, political, and intellectual problems con-
fronting modern society. Paradoxically, the universalism of
Picón Salas did not contradict his essential Americanism.
Inherent in the peregrination from the particular to the
universal is the element of return, or reintegration. To become
more universal in outlook did not mean, for the essayist, to
become less involved with the problems of Venezuela. Picón
Salas interpreted the particularity of circumstance as an
individual expression of the universal conception of life.
Identity, either personal or of the nation, could not develop
fully in the world without an awareness of a more general
and universal knowledge of world events. Universality, in
Picón Salas, identified what was general in many particular
circumstances. In this respect the pattern of life and the
development of his essayistic style parallels the work of other
twentieth-century essayists: Arturo Uslar Pietri, Alfonso
Reyes, and Pedro Henríquez Ureña, for example.

We must understand at this point that the theme of peregrination in Picón Salas is not unique, neither in the context of
Venezuelan literature nor in the context of Latin American
literature. Beginning with the chronicles of Hernán Cortés
and Bernal Díaz del Castillo, one finds the theme of exploration
in the hope of discovering the utopia described in the chivalric

novels of Spanish literature. In the seventeenth century, the
theme of voyaging in search of fortune is exemplified in the
fictional account by Carlos de Sigüenza y Góngora, *Infortunios
de Alonso Ramírez* (*The Misfortunes of Alonso Ramírez*). In
the eighteenth century, such wandering develops in the pica-
resque work of Alonso Carrió de la Vandera, *Lazarillo de
ciegos caminantes* (*Lazarillo of Blind Walkers*). The
nineteenth-century Mexican novelist, José Joaquín Fernández
de Lizardi, recreated in *El Periquillo Sarniento* (*The Scratch-
ing Parrot*) the theme of the *pícaro*, or rogue, setting out into
the world on a voyage of discovery.

After independence, the concept of peregrination joins with
the theme of exile in Spanish American literature. In José
Mármol's *Cantos de peregrino* (*Songs of the Voyager*) we
discover an autobiographical account of an author forced
into exile because of his opposition to the dictatorship of
Juan Manuel Rosas in Argentina. The Cuban poet José
María Heredia captures the longing for homeland in *Himno
del desterrado* (*The Hymn of the Exiled*). In *Facundo* by
Domingo Faustino Sarmiento, and in *Martín Fierro*, by
José Hernández, we discover a spirit of adventure and
wandering that traces a human trajectory from the plains
region to the urban center of the country. The nomadism in
Facundo and *Martín Fierro* has its parallel in the life-style of
the caudillos in Venezuela in the nineteenth century. Peregrination as an internal phenomenon in Latin American literature
results only in those countries of extensive land mass and
where a sharp division between rural and cosmopolitan
areas exists. The theme of wandering in countries such as
Argentina and Venezuela, involves the problems inherent in
social development and in domesticating the land. Whereas in
the early nineteenth century the peregrination of the precursors of independence centered around the goal of establishing
political autonomy, in the latter part of the century this becomes a search for civilization.

Angel Rosenblat has suggested that the study of Venezuelan
literature might center around the theme of peregrination.
Picón Salas, in *Literatura venezolana,* characterized the
particular Venezuelan phenomenon of wandering as *errancia
venezolana* (a Venezuelan peregrination). For Picón, the
characteristic of nomadism was fundamental in the develop-

ment of the country's historical and cultural heritage. It was
due to *errancia* (a neologism created by the essayist out of
the verb *errar*, meaning to wander) that so many Venezuelans
were represented in the Wars of Independence in Colombia,
Ecuador, and Peru. According to Picón, under the dictatorial
rule of Monagas, Guzmán Blanco, Castro and Gómez (the
latter two ruled Venezuela in the twentieth century) two
Venezuelas were created: the Venezuela possessed by the
forces of tropicalism and the rule of the caudillo dictators,
and an idealized Venezuela created by exiled intellectuals
opposed to the power of the caudillo.

III *The Venezuelan Experience*

With the exception of writers like Fermín Toro, Cecilio
Acosta, Juan Vicente González, and Gonzalo Picón Febres,
who make up the romantic era in Venezuelan literature, the
essay as a literary genre did not acquire national characteristics until scientific positivism had infiltrated the imagination
of men of letters. José Ramón Medina, in his history of
Venezuelan literature in the twentieth century, assessed the
influence of positivism on Venezuelan literature at the turn
of the century as follows:

Positivism, that new science which penetrates with evident delay
university studies of Venezuela, signifies a healthy impact for our
culture in general. The generation which controls this new attitude
of life possesses one of the genuine scientific positions in the country.
History, sociology, philosophy, and criticism enter into the world of
the Venezuelan essay with a new conception of life utilizing a method
of investigation not known to us before.[12]

According to Medina, positivism brought with it an interest in
studying, from a scientifically analytic point of view, the historical,
natural, and social phenomena of the country. In the unfinished work entitled "Flor caracasana" ("The Flora of Caracas"),
the German naturalist Adolfo Ernst, who immigrated to Venezuela
during the second half of the nineteenth century, opened the
door to a concern for the natural properties and resources of the
country.[13] The intellectual discipline that Ernst imposed on his
classes at Central University (Universidad Central de Venezuela)
demonstrated the use of scientific logic to a new generation of

Venezuelans. Ernst's methodology eventually led to a more comprehensive understanding of Venezuela's physical and intellectual reality. Guillermo Korn has suggested that Ernst's concern for the Venezeuelan flora also created an interest in the modernist movement for the search for the fundamental elements of creole culture.[14]

Luis Beltrán Guerrero points out that the positivist interpretation of history had a two-fold development in Latin America. One was the evolutionary approach to history which offered an organic interpretation of the order of life and events in the country. The other followed Montesquieu's principle that the laws of life are the relationships between things observable in nature. Applied to history, this means that history must be judged in accordance with · events observable in the course of time rather than as events following a pattern established by nature. Beltrán says that the historical interpretation of positivism which sought to discover the authentic relationships between the different elements of life in Latin America began with the ideas of Bolívar. Beltrán calls the positivism of the Venezuelan liberator an authentic positivism ("el positivismo auténtico"),[15] for in Bolívar there is inherent a concept of primordial cause which leads nations to determine their particular form of government. Each form of government is the result of a particular set of circumstances visible in the social character of the people. Beltrán indicates that Bolívar denied the existence of a philosophy of history as evident in the work of St. Augustine and G. W. F. Hegel. However, this does not preclude in the ideology of the Liberator a certain spiritualism and the hope of the positive evolution of the history of mankind. For Bolívar and his teacher Simón Rodríguez, the intellectual emancipation of Latin America was predicated on the capacity of the people to identify the problems of the continent. Latin America was more than a mere continuation of the traditions of Western civilization;[16] it possessed a political and cultural authenticity all its own.

Bolivar's authentic positivism, indicates Beltrán, influenced intellectuals in Venezuela more than the scientific positivism introduced in the continent toward the latter part of the nineteenth century. In a teacher and intellectual like Rafael Villavicencia, who subscribed to the concept of the discovery of the laws of life, there existed a comprehension of the spiritual underpinning evident in the history of a country. Similar to Bolívar,

Villavicencia believed in the interaction between the material and spiritual elements of life. According to Beltrán, Villavicencia argued that science seeks to harmonize faith and reason.[17] Significant in the thought of Villavicencia, was the concept that power, in time, becomes subordinate to the authority of wisdom and virtue. This idea of the intellectual progression of the course of history, as we shall see, repeats itself in Mariano Picón Salas.

Scientific positivism in Venezuela did not solve any of the problems that had plagued the nation from the beginning of the first Republic. It did, however, point out some of the salient issues that were to be the concerns of many of the literary Generation of 1918 and almost all writers of the Generation of 1928. These problems were: the intolerance that characterized the Wars of Federation, the question of centralism in government, the structure of the educational institutions in Venezuela, the significance of evolutionary Darwinism in interpreting the course of human development and history, and the struggle between the government of personalism, as manifested in the authority of the caudillo, and the concept of social progress.

IV   *The Generation of 1918*

The first group of Venezuelan writers to be considered an authentic generation in search of the proper literary form to express the identity of the nation was the Generation of 1918. Some of the poets and prose writers who made up this generation were Andrés Eloy Blanco, Paz Castillo, and Luis Enrique Mármol. Their principal goal, says José Ramón Medina, was to discover the authenticity of Venezuela ("la authenticidad venezolana").[18] The Generation of 1918 sought to transcend the forms and poetic destiny of the previous generation of modernist poets. They wanted to rise above the localism of the romantic poets of the nineteenth century and to express what they thought were the real problems of political and social life. They sought a balance between the literary content of national problems and a universal poetic form exemplified in the work of the Spanish writer Antonio Machado. Medina considers this generation a precursor to the Generation of 1928, which was more fully committed to solving the political problems of Venezuela; the Generation of 1928 often participated in the formation of political parties. In dealing with the authentic reality of Venezuelan circumstance, they began to internalize external existence in order to understand better the roots of the national poetic phenomena. With the Generation of 1918 there began to develop in Venezuela an awareness of the unity between the particularity of circumstance and the universal concept of form, and between ideas and aesthetics: "It was a poetry made of the embers of ideas, similar to the piercing tones of chamber music." [19]

V   The Generation of 1928

The desire to integrate literary expression with the circumstances of life in Venezuela crystallized as the nucleus of the literature of the Generation of 1928. For the most part, the writers of this generation adopted a positive view of the progressive characteristics inherent in the history and cultural traditions of the country.

The Generation of 1928 was influenced by the work of a nineteenth-century historian and sociologist, José Gil Fortoul (1862–1941), who incorporated into his work a sense of intuitionism and spiritualism that diverged from the negative positivism of a writer like César Zumeta. For Zumeta, the ills of Venezuela and the rest of the continent were organic in nature; he agreed with the Bolivian writer Alcides Arguedas in *El continente enfermo* (*The Sick Continent*), that the continent was in the process of living out its final days. The essayists of the Generation of 1928, which included writers like Felipe Massiani, Juan Oropesa, Mariano Picón Salas, and Arturo Uslar Pietri, nurtured a more positive vision of society. These writers established as their principal objective the unification of the heterogeneous elements of the nation. They discovered in Fortoul's *El hombre y la historia* (*Man and History*), a sense of historical progress; they substituted the intuitionism of Henri Bergson and Emile Boutroux for the deterministic elements of scientific positivism. From Bergson, the Generation of 1928 learned how to deal with the traditional concepts of time and space as conditions of the mind and spirit.[20]

Characteristic of the writers of the Generation of 1928 was an awareness of the essay as a literary form. Unlike the essayists and historians of the late nineteenth century, the Generation of 1928 attempted to define the problems of the country while keeping in mind the aesthetic attributes of literature. Furthermore, they did not seek to propagandize their ideas in the name of any political faction. There was an attempt to raise the fundamental truths about Venezuela and Latin America to the level of public consciousness. It was the view of the Generation of 1928 that the people of Venezuela were too much unaware of their identity as a united people with one common heritage. The essayists of 1928 relied on their own personal interpretation and intuition, as well as historical data, in expressing their concerns for the country. Whereas the prose writers of the latter part of the nineteenth century considered their task to be the historians of Venezuela, the essayists of 1928 thought themselves to be men of literature dealing with the facts of history.

Picón Salas' literary career belongs to two generations. One, the literary Generation of 1928; the other, a more loosely defined Generation of 1920 composed of intellectuals from the Andean town of Mérida, who in Caracas discovered the dichotomy between social reality and cultural ideas. Mariano Picón Salas represented an innovative spirit. In his constant wanderings Picón Salas struggled to understand the underlying reasons and legends of the rustic and traditional way of life in Mérida and in Latin America in general. The search for authenticity in the essayist's personal life and in the life of the nation was, as stated by Angel Rosenblat, a search for the authenticity of American traditions.[21]

VI   *Status of Criticism on Venezuelan Literature*

Until recently, Venezuelan literature and culture have received scant treatment from scholars both within and outside of the country. During the first part of the twentieth century, only four major works on Venezuelan literature were published, two in Venezuela, one in Spain, and one in the United States. In Venezuela, Fortoul published *Literatura venezolana* (1903), and the historian Gonzalo Picón Febres published *Historia de la literatura venezolana en el siglo diez y nueve* (1906).[22] Marcelino Menéndez y Pelayo included an extensive analysis of Venezuelan poetry in the nineteenth century in his compendium, *Historia de la poesía hispanoamericana* (1911). Finally, in 1933 Dillwyn Ratcliff published his doctoral dissertation under the title *Venezuelan Prose Fiction*. Ratcliff's work had a special interest at the time, for the study was the first succinct compilation of Venezuelan prose and it traced the development of that genre from the nineteenth century through to the time the dissertation was written.

The contemporary author who has received most recognition from students of literature is Rómulo Gallegos. Consistently Gallegos has been the object of monographic studies both in his country and outside.[23] Other writers of the twentieth century who have achieved international recognition are Andrés Eloy Blanco, Rufino Blanco Fombona, Manuel Díaz Rodríguez, Mariano Picón Salas, Arturo Uslar Pietri, and Venezuela's most famous woman writer, Teresa de la Parra. In the previous century, three writers who had received considerable recognition were Cecilio Acosta, Andrés Bello, and Simón Bolívar. Traditionally, Bello has not been treated as a Venezuelan intellectual because of the writer's errant life-style. Since Bello spent so much time in Chile, many critics link his name with the development of intellectualism in that country. Luis Alberto Sánchez, for example, in *Nueva historia de la literature americana* (*New History of Latin American Literature*), discusses the importance of Andrés Bello in terms of the developing Chilean cultural reality of the nineteenth century.[24]

In 1971 Domingo Miliani observed the following relationship between the literary marketplace and the production of literature in Venezuela:

> The lack of a vital internal market and of a national book industry has deprived great authors from being able to depend exclusively on their literary creation for their livelihood . . . books in Venezuela have been limited to small editions for local consumption. Writers have been obliged to publish their works in diverse literary periodicals which makes circulation difficult. These factors have caused an isolation of our literature in relation to the rest of Hispanic America.[25]

As we can see, Miliani's observation indicates a paucity of literary creation and criticism in Venezuela. One of the first to point this out was Mariano Picón Salas in 1940:

> There has not been written, and most assuredly for some time to come there will not be written, a history of our literature which exhausts its themes either through the investigation of documents or adequate criticism. Few men like the meritorius Manuel Segundo Sánchez have begun to organize our dispersed bibliography; few

institutions like the National Library and the Academy of History have cataloged their collections.[26]

Perhaps, as indicated by Miliani, the difference between the development of literature and literary criticism in Venezuela and in Mexico is to be found in the differences between these two countries' histories. In Mexico there exists a cultural tradition that includes the names of the great Aztec emperors Nezahual-coyotl and Montezuma; in Venezuela the names of the pre-Columbian chieftains, Sorocaima, Tamanaco, Guaicaipuro, Paramaconi, and Tiuna, do not conjure up memories of past glories in the minds of contemporary Venezuelan writers. When the Spaniards reached Mexico they discovered a sedentary and highly sophisticated civilization; in Venezuela the indigenous tribes were nomadic and easily subdued by the conquistadors. From colonial times up to the modern age, Venezuelans have re-tained a cultural concept determined by European patterns. The indigenous elements of the country have always been classified as barbaric. In Mexico, on the other hand, there has developed a concept of cultural fusion that incorporates both indigenous and Spanish elements. Mexicans have not nurtured an inferiority complex with regard to their cultural heritage as has occurred in Venezuela.

This sense of cultural inferiority alone does not explain the paucity in Venezuelan literature and criticism. The protracted period of the reign of the caudillo dictators and the prolonged period of civil strife in the nineteenth century also interfered with the creation of an extensive literary development. As indicated in the body of this study, there was created during the period of *caudillismo* the phenomenon of two Venezuelas: the Venezuela of the caudillos, and that of the intellectuals who fled the tyranny to other Latin-American countries. Many of these intellectuals and writers were published in literary periodicals during the last part of the nineteenth century and the first thirty years of the twentieth.

In the introduction to *Literatura venezolana*, Picón Salas recog-nized the element of a divided country as responsible for the con-temporary lack of knowledge concerning Venezuela's literary heritage. He stated the need to begin extensive research into the activity of the intellectuals and writers that lived in exile .

because of the ruthlessness of Venezuela's dictators and the imposition of censorship. However, one must not be left with the impression that the development of letters ceased as a creative function during the dictatorships of Antonio Guzmán Blanco, Cipriano Castro, and Juan Vicente Gómez. As pointed out by José Ramón Medina in *50 años de literatura venezolana* (*Fifty Years of Venezuelan Literature*), during the late nineteenth century and early twentieth, a literary tradition was established in the publication of literary periodicals. The problem was one of dissemination. For the most part, these periodicals were known only to the writers themselves. Before the emergence of the Generation of 1918, it is safe to say that writers wrote for themselves and that a literary public did not exist.

The first essayist of the twentieth century to provide Venezuelans with a critical analysis of their literary development from colonial to modern times was Mariano Picón Salas in *Literatura venezolana*, or *Formación y proceso de la literatura venezolana* (*Formation and Process of Venezuelan Literature*). Previous studies in the nineteenth and twentieth centuries did not offer the same kind of gestaltlike cultural insights as we discover in the work of Picón Salas. They were either in the nature of partial analysis, as in the study by Gonzalo Picón Febres' *Historia de la literatura venezolana en el siglo diez y nueve (ensayo de historia-crítica)* (*History of Venezuelan Literature in the XIX Century, a Historical-Critical Essay*, 1906); anthologies like *Nuevos poetas venezolanos* (*New Venezuelan Poets*, 1939) by R. Olivares Figueroa and *Parnaso venezolano* (*Venezuelan Parnassus*, 1892), by Julio Calcaño; or bibliographic lists as found in *Biblioteca de escritores venezolanos* (*Bibliography of Venezuelan Writers*, 1875) by José María Rojas. The closest in interpretative quality to the work by Picón Salas was the study by Luis López Méndez entitled *Mosáico de política y literatura* (*Mosaic of Politics and Literature*, 1891). The difference between López Méndez and Picón Salas resides in the former's preoccupation with the relationship between literature and Venezuelan political phenomena of the nineteenth century. Whereas López Méndez concentrated on investigating the schism in the political life of the country in terms of its influence on literature, Picón Salas sought to reconcile the dualism in Venezuelan political and cultural life by tracing the development of a unified national expression in literature beginning with the colonial period and concluding with the work of

Rómulo Gallegos. Picón Salas' intention in *Formación y proceso de la literatura venozolana* is summed up in the introduction. He declared the moral obligation of the man of letters to be thus:

To create a nation is for Venezuelans in this day and age to unite its disperse parts, to establish a possible area of agreement between generations antagonistic to one another. If beyond its mere informative value this brief history had any other intention, it would be to search through books and the lives of men the moral heritage which has yet to become a reality in our nation. To do this is not for mere erudition nor for its ornamental value, but, rather, to search for the vitality of life, the vigorous nature of our art, the hope and destiny of our people.[27]

CHAPTER 2

Mariano Picón Salas: Essayist

SINCE the publication of Montaigne's essays (*Essais*) in 1580, the difficulty in literary study has been to come to terms with the essay as a literary genre. Until recently, the term essay applied to almost any kind of treatise about a particular subject. The study of the essay has treated, almost exclusively, the subject matter contained. The problem has been that in dealing with the essay it has been difficult to discern between what Stender-Petersen called fictive and nonfictive language.[1] In Latin American literature, a truly systematic literary analysis of the essay has been done by James Willis Robb in his doctoral dissertation "Patterns of Image and Structure in the Essays of Alfonso Reyes," later translated into Spanish and published as *El estilo de Alfonso Reyes* (*The Style of Alfonso Reyes*). Robb demonstrated the unique literary style of Reyes. He concentrated his study on the development of the Reyian metaphor and adjective; in Reyes both metaphor and adjective contributed to the creation of a particular aesthetic vision of reality.

José Luis Martínez defined the essay as the expression of one man's sensitivity to the world around him. The essay, as a literary genre, is the result of a desire to express a personal vision of the world.[2] Less intuitive is the definition offered by Robert Mead. For Mead, the essay is a prose work that is general in nature and relatively brief in its extension.[3] Carlos Ripoll leans toward a psychological definition of the essay as opposed to a technical one: the essay is the result of the writer's desire to transmit in an artistic way the reflections and conclusions of personal experience within a particular circumstance.[4] Alberto Zum Felde recognizes in the first volume of his critical history of Latin American literature, *Indice crítico de la literatura latinoamericana* (*A Critical Index of Latin-American Literature*), the existence of the essay

34

as a union between intuition and erudition, between emotion and intellectualization.

In his interpretation of the essay, Antonio de la Nuez refers to what he calls *ensayismo*, or a state of mind necessary as a prerequisite for the essay to be created. For this critic, the various categories that have been used to classify the essay, like political essay or philosophical essay, are unimportant. What is essential to de la Nuez is that the essay ought to be viewed from the standpoint of the search for objective truth. The truth and logic of the essay are contained within the form itself. Truth is nothing but the image of reality conveyed by the essayist. The function of the essay is to discover a logic of reality not readily perceived in science or in history. The genre is created when the conclusions drawn in the essay can be distinguished from the elements of cause and effect apparent in the spatiotemporal reality of history. The essay, even when dealing with past events, attempts to project, through the intuition of the artist, a vision of the future.[5]

I   *Theory of the Essay in Picón Salas*

The historical and cultural functions of literature are more important to Mariano Picón Salas than the technical aspects that differentiate one genre from the other. He did recognize the existence of three fundamental genres—poetry, the novel, and the essay—and interpreted their functions as quests to explain and come to terms with the enigma and confusion of life and its problems. For Picón Salas each genre demonstrates a particular relationship between the artist and his environment. The three genres together, viewing reality from different perspectives, provide man with the idea that it is possible to resolve human problems and to escape from the labyrinth of life that limits the capacity of the individual to develop and progress: "If the life of man is a kind of labyrinth in which one must make a decision and even help others to search the roads of their conscience, we could then say that in the three fundamental literary forms of poetry, the novel and the essay there is expressed the special life experience of an earthbound Dedalus."[6]

For Picón Salas, the function of the poet, with his virtue and imagination, is to internalize the reality of the universe and to offer it back to the world in a lyrical and aesthetic form. The poet represents the plight of the individual suffering and hoping for a

better world. The novelist, in his objectivity, explains the concrete
relationships between men. His function is to indicate the circumstances of life and the particular problems that have created the
labyrinth of existence. Unlike the poet, who deals with universal
concepts of pathos, joy, and beauty, the novelist represents these
elements in the particular world of his characters. The function of
the essayist is to extend a bridge between the world of images and
philosophical concepts. The essayist attempts to resolve conflict
in the pursuit of harmony, which he achieves by synthesizing the
conditions of the adversaries involved in conflict. Similar to the
novelist, the essayist deals with particular circumstances. Unlike
the novelist, the essayist has the obligation to direct the individual in escaping from the labyrinth. Consequently, the essayist
must concern himself with action: the essay is not merely con-
templative.[7]

Picón Salas interpreted the essay in Latin America as an exhortative genre in the style of Domingo Faustino Sarmiento and
other essayists of the nineteenth century who sought to educate
their societies regarding the social and political conditions and
who attempted to reconcile the conflict between civilized society
and the chaos evident in the political life of the continent. In
Picón Salas, reconciliation is a form of action. The exhortation
called for by Picón Salas was not to be political propagandization
of the masses through partisan rhetoric. The formula of the essay,
as with other genres, he said, is to say something that will stimulate the conscience of men and awaken in them their emotions.
The measure of an authentic and socially relevant literature can
be determined by the degree with which the artist unites the
literary elements of ideas and emotion. As Picón stated, authenticity can only exist "when the work of art offers not only the
machinery for the dreams of artists but a language which moves
the emotions of other men as well."[8] To illustrate what he was
talking about, he cited Plato, Voltaire, Cervantes, and Unamuno.[9]
These were the models to be followed by the writer setting out to
raise the level of social awareness in the general population.

What Picón Salas admired was an ability to describe the authentic relationships between cultures. In the particular case of
Sarmiento, the cultural relationship described was between a
technologically expanding European culture and a more under-
developed Latin American one:

He was a writer who wished to diminish the technical and moral distances which separate us from Europe, and who put into his *Facundo*, a book which does not have any precise literary classification: the sociology and novelistic elements, history and the typology of America bursting at the seams. It is a book which might even frighten Europeans accustomed to distinguishing the various literary genres and defining the rational frontiers of thought. Yet in its apparent disorder—similar to poetry dealing with the cosmos—it contains the conscience and the subconscience of Hispanic American life.[10]

Picón Salas saw in the essay a particular relationship between the existence of the genre and historical time. The essay, he said, in its intermediary role between the lyrical expression of poetry and the ideas of philosophy, develops in time of crisis. Since the essay possesses a more direction oriented characteristic than the other two genres, it establishes itself as literature during moments of historical and cultural transition. The essay addresses the confusion of men at a time when old cultural values seem to be crumbling in the advance of a new value structure: "Due to its very nature, the essay developed during periods of crisis, when man felt most confused and when the traditional values of culture were being threatened and started to crumble." [11]

The essayist, directly concerned with real circumstances, is subject to the events of history and must await the moment for social, political, and cultural problems or crises to present themselves before he can exercise his literary function. Picón Salas compared the relationship between the essayist and the problems mentioned to the experiments of Issac Newton. Problems must fall at the feet of the essayist before he can deal with them: "The essayist writes when an apple [the apple, here, is a metaphor for human problems] falls at his feet, and when, with his developed sense of smell, like that of a hunter, and the sensitivity of a poet, he becomes aware that something is going to happen and is happening." [12]

The meaning of the foregoing strikes at a major difference between the novelist and the essayist. Whereas the novelist describes events, or circumstances, whether or not crisis exits in the society, the essayist must define situations that trouble men. Referring to his own talents as a writer, Picón Salas had the following to say: "To define problems, even though definition seems a bit unusual to those who comment on life on a daily basis, has been for me the hard purpose of the writer. I would like to insist on this purpose in spite of any criticism in favor of or against me." [13]

One of the essayist's tasks, then, is to decide what is a problem and what is not. In Picón Salas, the use of the word "problem" in describing the themes of the essay presented a semantic difficulty. He thought that the essayist must discern between major and minor problems within the society and set himself the goal of dealing with only the major ones. The situations of everyday occurrence were not suitable themes for the essayist. To discuss, for example, a particular difficulty created by the political establishment might be the task of newspaper editorials, but they were not the problems to be treated in essays. The essayist, however, must define the underlying cultural and social currents that have created difficult situations, that have created dictatorships, and must deal with broad universal concepts.

Cultural, historical, and social difficulties require long-term solutions. But first these difficulties must be defined by the essayist. As Picón Salas stated:

I confess my aversion for the word "problem," a beseiged and somewhat enigmatic word if it is not understood well. It is a word which when pronounced appears to swallow up all other explanations and for that reason it is a favorite of those who can explain nothing. It is a word which is being used a lot in Venezuela, especially during the last four years—that is to say, since that moment in which we were allowed to express our opinions and to write freely [Picón Salas is referring, here, to the death of the dictator Juan Vicente Gómez]. It is as if through this word we have been able to identify all that is missing in the country. [14]

In the work of Picón Salas, the main issue, as he reviewed the historical past, was not the problem of *caudillismo* as a particular phenomenon in the regimes of Cipriano Castro or Juan Vicente Gómez. *Los días de Cipriano Castro*, for example, transcends the particularities of life under the dictator. The dictator himself represents an historical phenomenon of the struggle between barbarism and civilization, or the lack of culture.

The element of crisis that acts as a stimulus in the work of Picón Salas is both personal and historical, particular and universal. It is a multilevel crisis of the personal struggle for identity and the search for authenticity within Venezuela and Latin America. External problems are internalized and the essayist seeks to transmit to others the feeling of anguish rising out of the crisis in culture. Picón Salas interpreted the crisis of the twentieth century to be, in Orteguian terms, the dehumanization of Western man: a spiritual and moral crisis. According to the essayist, the justification of his work, and for that matter all literature, was to be found in its ability to communicate a sense of the twentieth-century crisis to the rest of society: "I believe that the major joy and justification of all literary works is to speak to the unknown reader, to our unknown brothers and comrades who can sense our anguish and who will think about those ideas which we toss out to the mercy of the wind." [15] By anguish, or *angustia*, Picón Salas meant a critical awakening or a nonacceptance of static ideology or provincial *Weltanschauung*.

A member of the Venezuelan Generation of 1928, Picón Salas sought to consolidate, in his literary theories, the apparent antithetical position of the modernist advocacy of art for art's sake vis-à-vis social realism in literature. Neither school, he thought, focused in on the proper relationship between art and society and the duties of the writer: "No school of art has value in itself, and the bad imitator of Mallarmé is as unworthy of our support, from an artistic point of view, as the author of cumbersome and vile narrations in the naturalist mode." [16] The error of both schools of literary theory was, according to Picón Salas, that their positions had become fossilized by their adoption of an ideological approach to literature: each had failed to understand the condition of art as a fluid and interactive expression of the relationship between artist and object. When an artist intentionally avoids contact with what he considers to be a repulsive, materialistic, bourgeois world, he consciously or unconsciously expresses a social attitude. On the other hand, when a naturalist or social realist attempts to avoid contact with the aesthetic nature of literature, he fails as an artist.[17] The main concern of both modernist and naturalist had been with the ends of art rather than with the means: "In both cases the problem in literature, is not so much for what reason it is written, but 'how' the work is produced." [18] The search for authenticity in literature is an ever-evolving process dependent on rhythm, language, and emotion—elements that ought to be governed by a sense of disinterest and compassion for the changing moods and structures of society. Picón Salas stated that the advocates of art for art's sake had converted literature into a sport and had succeeded in isolating the intellectual from the problems

of society and culture.[19] The social realists demonstrated a lack
of a sense of literary authenticity by subordinating art to scientific
disciplines and political propaganda.

Picón Salas saw literature as a cultural phenomenon responsible
for interpreting history spiritually. In literature the struggle for
justice is intricately tied in with the search for beauty and aesthetic values. While literature cannot avoid contact with the society,
it, at the same time, cannot be projected as subordinate to the
historical moment. It must reflect the past and the present and
must project a vision of the future. The aesthetic nature of literature resides in the way in which it projects such an image. The
writer must perceive the dimension of time synchronically and
distill from that vision a concept of the authentic cultural con-
figuration of reality. For Picón Salas, the Chilean writer Gabriela
Mistral represented a prime example of the harmonious relationship between the technical aspects of literature and the search
for cultural authenticity: "And so it is that Gabriela represented
. . . a unique expression of Hispanic American sensitivity and
conscience. Not only did her poems, after the superficial excesses
of modernism, bring to the lyric quality of our language an
authentic expression of the vigor of life—an existential testimony
—such as had not been witnessed since the time of the mystics in
Spain, but her literature—conquering the erotic and sentimental
expression of feminist poetry of a previous age—set out to conquer
new horizons of human experience." [20]

II   *The Search for Authenticity in Picón Salas*

For our author the search for national cultural authenticity or
Venezolanidad developed with the notion that in Venezuela there
did not exist a harmony between the form of literature and its content. On the other hand, life in Mérida did represent a form of
cultural authenticity for Picón Salas. In the province there existed
a harmonious relationship between nature, the literary content,
and the life of the people. People in Mérida knew their identity;
they held to their traditions, and from their traditions they developed a concept of the world that sustained their way of life for
generations. The cultural problem in Mérida in the twentieth
century was that the traditional way of life was being invalidated
by the influence of an outside world unsympathetic to those traditions. While it is true that Picón Salas sought to rediscover the

traditions of the past, it is also true that he searched for a way to revitalize those traditions in concert with the needs and demands of a changing world. Hence, the search for authenticity, paralleling the author's interpretation of the fluid movement of history, becomes a search for personal and cultural identity. Yet, this question does not exist in isolation from the realities of the external world. Both authenticity or identity involve the understanding of life as an interaction between particular mores and universal ethical values: "Countries like people only prove their value and significance in contact, contrast, and analogy with others. And it is because of this fervent desire to present that which is typically Venezuelan within the general current of universal history—our responsibility to counter many myths and prejudices—that I have encountered many hardships in my career as a writer." [21] If a traditional society can be considered authentic in terms of the relationship between its people and their traditions, it does not follow that there exists an authentic relationship between that society and the rest of the world. Venezuela and Latin America could not resurrect the colonial traditions, nor, as Francisco Miranda wanted to do in the nineteenth century, reestablish the supremacy of Inca civilization in a technological world demanding that these traditions be jettisoned for more democratic and materialistic values. At the same time, Picón Salas saw the substitution of old cultural values by new ones as a cause for anxiety. What the essayist wanted to do was to mold the external influences of the world to fit the particular identity of Venezuela and Spanish America.

The quest for authenticity imposed upon the author a sense of civic duty to discover the true identity of the cultural history of Venezuela. He said, "One writes about the nation in a state of tension, beseiged by problems and as a form of civic duty rather than as art." [22] His literary intention was to avoid polemicizing the history of Venezuela. In *Odisea de tierra firme* (*Odyssey on Land*), he stated this intention very clearly: "Without being a polemical work nor a political tract, it is a work of a poetic nature in which there is reflected the turbulent emotional image of the nation. The author evokes an image of the countryside and of those who have passed away. In general it conjures up time past." [23]

In describing the pattern of social nomadism created out of the fierce rivalries between the various *caudillos* vying for power,

Picón Salas does not set up a moral construct in which the forces of evil oppose the forces of good. The book is descriptive of a period of unrest and attempts to show the interrelationship between human activity and the nature of the land. To seek out the authenticity of Venezuelan culture meant for the essayist the acquisition of knowledge about the internal reality of life in the country and the perception of that life in the minds of the people:

> Venezuela with its rivers and people, its tropics and paradises, the dreams of its multitudes, the experience of its mestizo race, the lands yet to be discovered, and the music of its land is a theme too great for a single poet to undertake. The truly great Venezuelan poet will be one who, in spite of literary formulas and present rhetorical conventions, will be able to submerge himself in all this material. He will be able to express the mystery that lies within us. His song will coincide with the spirit of our collective soul and his words will express that revelation which we are all waiting for.[24]

I stated earlier that the search for authenticity in Picón Salas was motivated by the essayist's sense of an existing personal and national alientation from the reality of life; and I have also indicated Picón's view of the modernists' alienation from society. Part of the intellectual problem of twentieth-century man was a feeling of alienation, or lack of authenticity. The existentialist writers later represented this universal alienation in their sense of ennui and nausea. For Picón Salas, alienation was tantamount to a feeling of nihilism. His own anxieties and sense of anguish with regard to civilization and life opposed the essential thesis of the existentialist writers that life was a solitary and inexplicable journey. According to him, the nihilism of the existentialist was due to a total dissatisfaction with the circumstances of life and the idea that very little could be done to change the situation that prompted the feelings of ennui and nausea. Consequently, for Picón Salas, the existentialist way of viewing life was static and fatalistic. He saw the acquisition of a concept of authenticity as a positive goal toward the liberation of the individual from ennui and nausea.[25]

III   *The Significance of* Errancia *or Peregrination*

Our essayist understood the concept of *errancia* not only as a mere wandering or movement of people across the vast expanses of the Venezuelan countryside, but also as part of the legendary and historical course of societal and intellectual development that had its roots in the mythology of Greek literature. The concept of odyssey is more than a simple metaphor in his work. It entails, as in the voyage of Ulysses, a movement toward the unknown in search of Utopian dreams. Picón Salas discovered the existence of the idealistic element of Latin American peregrination in the pattern of life of the precursors of Venezuelan Independence. In *Regreso de tres mundos* (*Return from Three Worlds*), he identified Francisco de Miranda as the ancestor of all Venezuelans in search of liberty and utopia: "He was a kind of great-great-grandfather of all wandering Venezuelans who have searched outside of their native land for the freedom that they lacked and who have created a utopialike vision of their country, the product of their dreams and their nostalgia." [26]

Another author, Pedro Emilio Coll, also interpreted the existence of a nomadic spirit in Venezuela as fundamental to understanding the nature of the Venezuelan psyche. For Coll, the spirit of peregrination as discovered in Simón Bolívar represented the desire of the individual to join forces with the changing forms of nature: "Bolívar wanted to appear, through his words, not like the trees which root themselves forever in the land, but like the wind, the water, the sun, and all other things that move and change without end." [27]

As a description of social phenomenon, *errancia*, in Picón Salas, becomes an element in comprehending the cultural identity of the Spanish American or *criollo* after independence. The essayist seized upon the view of the wandering *criollo* as a constant in the cultural history of the continent. Different from the wandering nomadic tribesman, who inhabited the hemisphere in the pre-Colombian era, Picón Salas perceived the peregrination of the *criollo* in terms of a circular design: the movement of the nomadic tribesman was linear. For one reason or another, be it for the purpose of fulfilling the desires of an adventurous spirit or for political reasons, the pattern of life of the *criollo* was a movement away from and back to the center of his existence. The axis around which this movement revolves presents in the life of the *criollo* a conflict between a world within and a world without. One pole of the axis represents the spirit of adventure that motivated the *criollo* to remove himself from the center of his existence, the land in which he grew up, and the other pole represents, as we shall see in the life and work of Picón Salas, the need to reintegrate himself, after a time, with the very environment that previously seemed to inhibit the full development of his individuality.

This circular movement of cultural *errancia* can be interpreted abstractly as the movement from the particular to the universal and back to the particular. For Picón Salas, *errancia* in the *criollo* is a factor that distinguishes Latin American from European man: "The Europeans who were born in the cradle of old civilizations, which were well organized, cannot understand this instinctive peregrination of the creole man, this continuous adventure similar to that of argonauts which we must understand in order to clarify the substance of our own reality." [28]

IV   Errancia *as a Quest*

Errancia, or peregrination, in the work of Picón Salas is the central design around which the essayist structures the development of his themes. Throughout the essays there is a constant pattern of movement from the world within to the world without, in terms of the relationship between the internal reality of Venezuela and the reality of life beyond its boundaries. The term *errancia* is synonymous with what the author called his peregrination through life (*P*, ix). It incorporates the two aspects of peregrination studied by Jurgen Hahn: the quest for some utopian external reality or paradise lost, and the quest for personal identity.[29]

The path of *errancia* is relatively simple. It extends from a point in the past filled with memories and traditions, passes through the present, and eventually leads to a perception of a different world of perfection: "Autobiography like the history of a nation is nothing more than the nostalgia of the world which we leave behind and the ardent sense of utopia, constantly being rectified and changed, for this other world which we would like to achieve." [30] Yet, the world of utopia sought by the author is not the allusive reality of a totally imaginary existence. It is a perception of the reality of this world as it can or ought to be. The path of *errancia* is one of hope, an aspiration of making the circumstances of reality better for the development of individual spirit. The trajectory of *errancia* in Picón Salas is both a physical one, as in the voyages made by the pilgrims of the fifteenth century, or as in the voyages of the argonauts of Greek literature, an intellectual one. The physical aspect of voyaging from Venezuela to other countries in Latin America, to Europe, and to the United States had the effect of cosmopolitanizing the spirit of the author and establishing in his literature themes of universal concern. From the standpoint of the author as an individual, the trajectory of *errancia* presents itself as a search for personal identity.

Paralleling Hahn's interpretation of *peregrinatio* in the fifteenth century, we discover in the work of Picón Salas, particularly in the later essays, the quest for the external-internal reality of a paradise lost. Externally, that reality is Venezuela and, in particular, the Andean mountain region of Mérida, where the author was born; internally, that reality represents, for the author, the fond memories of childhood when the world was filled with illusions. As can be seen, the need to rediscover or to reintegrate the self within the cultural circumstances of his homeland completes the trajectory of *errancia,* as mentioned previously, and determines its circular design. The quest for paradise lost is filled with the element of nostalgia, a consequence of life in exile. Similar to a linear search for utopia, the desire to rediscover the paradise of the past incorporates a utopian perception of life. This utopian perception of the past represents the author's dissatisfaction with the present condition of life. The search for paradise lost is an idealization of a period of time predating the advent of a consumer society. Once the author left his homeland in search for adventure, there developed a sense of disillusionment with reality that drew him back to contemplate the sedentary and bucolic life of Mérida. Reminiscing about his childhood, Picón Salas conjured up the following vision: "Even when I was a child in my mountain city I became acquainted with horse traders, men who worked in the fields and other people who struggled to make a living and who seemed to carry on the soles of their feet the description of the dirt roads, the smell of crushed grass, and the personal science connected with their knowledge of legends, proverbs and popular songs" (*P,* xiv).

When Picón Salas left Venezuela for Chile in 1923, Mérida was the citadel of conservatism. Life was relatively simple in Mérida and both the pattern of life of the people and the cyclical movement of nature seemed to complement one another. On the other hand, Caracas in the early twentieth century was developing a more varied life-style and a more materialistic value system in conjunction with the development of the nation as an industrial state. In part, Picón Salas' desire to leave Venezuela for Chile was motivated by the hope of discovering the essential cultural values of Spanish American society and the search for a way to preserve those values.

In Chile, Picón Salas soon discovered that consumerism and the material way of life were displacing the spiritualism of a prior history. While the barbarism of the dictatorships of the nineteenth century seemed to be waning in favor of the electoral process, he concluded that Latin America was being assaulted by another and more insidious form of cultural barbarism. The modern age, with its attendant industrialization, was introducing a value structure unsympathetic to the authentic and traditional values of Spanish America's cultural heritage. In 1955 Picón wrote a novel entitled *Los tratos de la noche* (*Night Deals*). The protagonist Alonso Segovia represented, for the author, the struggle between traditional values and the imported values of the present. Though the city of Caracas, the setting of the novel, is seen in a state of material and social change, it is evident that for the older members of the society such change represents confusion rather than human betterment.

For Picón Salas the materialistic ethic brought with it a value structure based on convenience and the exigencies of the present. The technology of the modern world and the demands that it created for material goods seemed to the essayist antithetical to the peace and harmony of the world. In a series of essays, *Los malos salvajes* (*The Evil Savages*), Picón surmised that technology was responsible for both World Wars: "The period which found a substitute for God in technology created the airplane, increased production in all areas, and improved means of communications. It did not give peace and serenity to man." [31]

Seen from the perspective of the foregoing discussion, the search for paradise lost is, in the work of the essayist, an attempt to counter the effects of cultural and spiritual disintegration. The rediscovery of the past and reintegration into the pattern of a more traditional way of life was a way of revitalizing the value system that was rapidly disappearing. In *De la conquista a la independencia* and in *Hispanoamérica, una posición crítica*, Picón Salas reinterpreted the past of Spanish America from the colonial period up through the period of independence, and concluded that the temporal relevancy of the past was in the effort of the conquistadors to establish a new world.

It must not be concluded that the search for paradise lost was solely an intellectual undertaking. The memory of Mérida, while the author was living in exile, created a longing for his homeland. Mérida became an aesthetic and emotional respite from the daily struggle to survive and the sociopolitical problems of the world:

> Born in Mérida, in the Andean mountain range of Venezuela, I finished my university studies in Chile. I returned to my homeland with my first grey hairs after the death of Juan Vicente Gómez, and, later, I moved to Europe, the United States, Mexico, and South America. I never forgot, however, my green Andean highlands with their snow-capped mountains through which the clearest of rivers break in torrents, and my old city, with its tucked eaves and bell towers, where, during the time of my youth, one lived with a sense of calm similar to that experienced during the eighteenth century of our colonial period." (*P*, ix)

In Venezuelan literature, an example of the wanderer in quest of personal salvation can be found in *Camino de perfección* (*The Perfect Way*), by the modernist novelist Manuel Díaz Rodríguez. Typical of the modernist movement in Latin America, the protagonist of the novel is unable to reconcile the differences between personal needs and the reality of political, social, and geographic conditions within the country. The only solution that the author can devise, as in the case of Lord Byron, is to escape the oppressiveness of Venezuelan reality and discover the internal utopia of self-realization: "Rather than to live in a land already conquered, I prefer to conquer my own terrain, even though it be that of the heavens, with my own hatchet and machete." [32] In Picón Salas there can also be found the need to establish personal identity. In his first book *Buscando el camino* (*A Search for a Way*), Picón indicated the importance of developing the integrity of self as follows: "There is nothing more curious in the history of the spirit than the search for a way." [33] The difference, however, between the discovery of self found in Byron and in Díaz Rodríguez, and that which can be seen in Picón Salas is the following. Whereas the discovery of self in the former represents an act of withdrawal from the reality of immediate circumstance, in Picón Salas the search for personal identity begins with a recognition of his cultural identity as a Venezuelan. To this extent, Mariano Picón Salas reflects the postmodernist movement in Venezuela that began with the Generation of 1918.

The emphasis in Picón Salas on the quest for personal identity is the search for the spiritual essence of self. In his literature, the spiritual essence of self is personified in the figure of a gardener, whom the author calls "mi ella." [34] The relationship between the author and "mi ella" is nearly mystical in nature. "Mi ella," whom the poet-essayist identifies as the incarnation of dreams and lyrical excesses, represents the ethical and aesthetic portion of self that strives to direct the expression of the author's ego. It represents the antithesis of sentimentalism and the total egocentric involvement with the senses discovered in the journeys of a Lord Byron. It is the spiritual force with whom the author constantly identifies in his struggle to achieve balance and harmony in life. If life is passion, as seen in the forces of nature, "mi ella" is the force of sublimation that seeks to resolve the conflict between reason and passion; it gives the author the strength to direct the forces of human passion, which he transforms into a metaphor of an unbroken pony: ". . . to domesticate as if it were a pony, this spirited colt which life is." [35]

The concern for proper conduct and ethical values in the quest for personal identity establishes in the essays of Picón Salas an immediate relationship between the author and his environment. His ethics are not personally defined, but come to the author from without. Yet while the ethical system that he accepts as part of his identity is Christian in nature, we must not make the mistake of assuming that the Christianity of Picón Salas consists of the lessons and tenets of behavior learned in catechism classes. What is important to Picón are the broad aspects of Christian civilization that has its roots in the Greek and Roman heritage. Significant to the value system of the essayist are the traditional concepts of brotherly love, the sublimation of passion in order to create great works of art and stable societies, the integrity of the individual as a spiritual entity, and the search for harmony among men.

Picón suggested that, perhaps, the type of individualism and sentimentalism evidenced in poets such as Lord Byron or in the modernist writers of Latin America can be tolerated in a country that already has established its cultural identity. In such a country the internal forces of society can be marshaled to counterbalance the excesses of individuals as they experience life; these societal forces, laws, traditions, and institutions can, in the long run, preserve the standards of behavior defied by individuals.[36] In Latin America, however, such individualism cannot be tolerated, since the identity of the continent had not yet been firmly established and the excesses of individual expression could only prolong the period of cultural insecurity. The essayist felt it necessary for the individual writer in Latin America to express his personal identity in terms of the discovery of a broader and more external national identity.

For our author the conflict between reason and passion in the individual manifests itself in the culture and society of Spanish America as a struggle between civilization and barbarism. The "unbroken pony" alluded to in the above quotation describes the turbulent conditions of life in the continent. If "mi ella," or the spiritual substance of life in the individual, has the function of ordering the garden of the artist's passions, Picón Salas sees his own literary function as one of creating a paradise of harmony out of the land itself ("la tierra de labrantío que es nuestra vía").[37]

Picón Salas set out on his literary career in quest of the illusive goals of a utopian ideal, glory, and love ("El ideal, La gloria, El amor"). The image conveyed in his first book is that of a young man in search of spiritual development. Adventurous and desirous to know the multifarious forms of reality, he embarked on a peregrination without any specific destination. His intention was to accumulate data and to internalize the various elements of physical reality: "I satisfy my spiritual need in gathering together these articles. It is the satisfaction of a wanderer who left without a compass, who found many highways, who carried a notebook, and who noted down what he saw." [38]

In the first essay, entitled "Vidas" ("Lives"), the author evokes the image of three types of individuals in search of self-realization. The first is a monk, who has the characteristics of a St. Francis of Assis. The monk, removed from the mainstream of life, has discovered how to harmonize the spiritual essence of his soul with the serenity of his natural environment. The second figure is that of the traditional Spanish *pícaro*, or rogue. The spirit of nonconformity and adventure found in the life of the *pícaro* represents for the essayist the more vital element in the

cultural characteristics of Spanish society. Third, we discover
the figure of a modernist bohemian, who in his preoccupation
with the sensual pleasures of life is compared to Lord Byron. All
of these individuals have one thing in common: to seek out a way
for self-fulfillment and self-realization in life.

The figure that most interests Picón Salas is that of the *pícaro*.
Between the total isolation of the monk and the rebellious de-
bauchery of the bohemian, the *pícaro* represents a middle
ground. The *pícaro*, not isolated from society and not totally
involved in seeking sensual pleasure, establishes a harmony
between spiritual and physical needs. Yet, each of the three
individuals depicted offer in their individuality a lesson for the
essayist himself. From the monk the author comes to understand
the importance of discipline and self-control. The bohemian
represents an intense love of life and teaches the author how to
transform spirit into a passion for existence: ". . . hacer de mi
espíritu un solo jardín de fiebre." [39] The lesson of the *pícaro* resides
in his spontaneity and nonconformity to established institutions.
As the *pícaro* represents a kind of middle ground between the
monk and the bohemian, in the life and work of the essayist
errancia transforms itself into a search for a balance between
the asceticism of the monk and the sensual involvement of the
bohemian.

In the essay "Pintura de un vivir" ("A Picture of Life"), Picón
Salas traces the spiritual development of a writer in three stages
of his existence: youth, maturity, and old age. The most important
period for the essayist is the period of maturity: "At thirty years
of age we ought to understand that we are no longer like wild
horses set loose in life. We ought to learn that there are reasons
for living beyond our individual pleasures—country, home,
world. At thirty years of age go forth to establish your home and
work with discipline. Establish your home. You are a man and
other men must be created." [40] For Picón Salas, the artist, in
order to bring to fruition all his talents, must commit himself to
his society and seek out solutions to problems. The peregrination
of Picón Salas is an attempt to seek solutions to the cultural
problems of Spanish America. The search for self possesses, along
with individual passion, a civic responsibility which the artist
cannot avoid: "We would be bad sons of this earth if we were to
isolate ourselves in our own intellectual niche and turn our backs
on people and their needs. Fortunately, we have not reached this

intellectually proud and inhuman position. For us art is not enough. We hope to share with others the multiple responsibility of having lived" (*P*, xv).

Mundo imaginario (*An Imaginary World*), a continuation of the author's search for personal identity, is a series of vignettes of a young man in search of independence. It is a book that reaches beyond the physical voyage to Chile and into the outer reaches of the author's imagination as he prepares to encounter the future. The essays depict the author's struggle to survive and his attempt to hang on to the illusions of youth. While the essayist seeks out the future, he retains a personal identification with traditional life in Mérida:

When I arrived at the town's railroad station to take the train, the train which was to put new lands and men between my past and my future, a train which represented fearful and new resolutions, the familiar sound of the pealing of bells came to me in the morning wind. They were clear and happy sounds of the church bell which announced to the people a baptism or a wedding, and all those cheerful events which add a note of joy and hope to the tightly drawn features of provincial people. How the sound of the bells disturbed me in that supreme moment when I was beginning to feel detached from everything and everybody. They were familiar sounds which were inviting me to stay. There among those blue mountains were my life and my destiny. There was the tranquil life and quiet destiny of those men who were my ancestors.[41]

The nature of the quest in Picón Salas is not a search for something that the artist or the nation did not possess. It is an examination of consciousness as defined by Ernesto Mayz Vallenilla in *El problema de América* (*The Problem of America*).[42] The *errancia* of Picón Salas is a process of arriving at an awareness or a consciousness of what America is all about.

CHAPTER 3

Toward a Quest for Identity

I A Cultural Orientation

MARIANO Picón Salas interpreted the discord in Latin American history since the time of independence as the loss of identity of the individual with the historical-cultural circumstance that began to develop with the dream of the first *conquistadores:* the dream of finding a new utopia in the New World. The independence gained through the efforts of Simón Bolívar was, according to Picón Salas, an attempt to bring to fruition this dream; it was a hope for the autonomous development of a new mestizo civilization as a counterpoise to a European culture that seemed to be growing old and tired. In the years that followed independence, the Bolivarian dream to unite the continent under the banner of Pan-Americanism vanished with the confrontation of that dream by the swarthy man on horseback, the caudillo, who roamed and ruled supreme in the plain areas of the continent. Picón interpreted the factionalism and fratricide that characterized the Latin American history of the second half of the nineteenth century and part of the early twentieth as the loss of spiritual and cultural values. Picón saw these values as having been substituted by the untamed forces of passion, thus creating an era of the predominance of barbarism over civilization.

The quest for identity in the life and work of Picón Salas was a voyage, an *errancia* as he called it, in search of the spiritual and cultural values inherent in the history of the continent. In his travels to various South American countries, the United States, and Europe, Picón Salas hoped to distill a vision of a new cultural synthesis that would inspire his fellow Latin Americans to redefine the position of Latin America in the world.

The essayist's *errancia* was, at the same time, a search for his own personal identity, first as a Venezuelan and, later, as a South American. For Picón Salas, there existed a symbiotic relationship between the history of country and the biography of the individual. Similar to Unamuno, the Venezuelan identified the life of the individual with that of the *infra-historia* of the country.[1] The individual is born into a society which, through language and traditions, gives him his basic identity; in turn the individual reaches beyond those traditions in an attempt to mold the society in accordance with the things he has learned through experience and education. The fundamental ingredient that sustains the vitality of life in both entities is the hope of reaching the ultimate goal of utopia. The *errancia* in the life of the individual and in the history of the country was, for Picón Salas, a linear ascent toward this goal. It must be remembered, however, that the course of history, similar to the pattern of life in the individual, was not considered by Picón Salas in terms of a deterministic philosophy of history. The voyage of *errancia*, as the author repeatedly experienced, was filled with disappointments. The antithesis of idealism is reality, which requires both the individual and the society to approach utopia through trial and error.

In the history of Venezuela, Picón Salas sought to comprehend what he called the process of Venezuelan thought ("el proceso del pensamiento venezolano"). Alfonso Reyes, in *Ultima Tule,* similarly considered the search for the cultural essence of America as the discovery of "la inteligencia americana." [2] For the Mexican essayist, acknowledging the existence of a spiritual entity in the continent meant perceiving a cultural unity that transcended the political disunity of Spanish America. The vision of Picón Salas was parallel to that of Reyes. For the most part, Picón said, Venezuelan historiography had failed to offer a vision of an *inteligencia venezolana.* Projecting a personal *errancia* through the Venezuelan past, the essayist hoped to dissolve the differences between the historical Cains and Abels. Yet, as an essayist rather than an historian, Picón was not intent on rewriting the history of Venezuela. Like Reyes, he employed the intuition of the essayist as artist in order to reach conclusions. He wanted to extract from the historical evidence of Venezuela, with its violence and hatred, the essence of Venezuela, or its so-called *venezolanidad.* In his study entitled *Literatura venezolana* (*Venezuelan Literature*), he stated that essence as "this short but fervent history of the Venezuelan soul." [3]

The path taken by Picón Salas in the discovery of his own
identity throughout the various stages of his life precipitated the
search for the cultural identity of Venezuela. In mid-life, he
said: "And here I am groping my way since adolescence in search
of that road leading to self actualization which will identify my
destiny, my work amongst men."[4] The question of destiny, here,
has the synchronic effect of interrelating the elements of historic
time—past, present, and future—with that of the author's own
life. The search for destiny in the work of Picón Salas requires a
journey into the historical past to discover the origin of personal
and national circumstance. The trajectory of Picon Salas' intellectual *errancia* in quest of identity began in his first book,
Buscando el camino, published in 1920.

II A Search for a Way

The collection of essays entitled *Buscando el camino* and all
subsequent writings prior to 1933 were intentionally omitted
from the author's personal anthology *Obras selectas*. Picón Salas
explained the reason for these omissions as a pruning from the
body of his work of those elements he thought to be the product
of youth and immaturity: "From my literary work I have supressed
for purposes of this anthology, the pages I wrote before 1933.
Those early essays that appear to me today to be exaggeratedly
verbose and not pruned of the pedantry of youth. It seems that
in them I became involved in trying to demonstrate how bright
I was" (*P*, ix). The illusion created by this statement is that it is
possible to divide the work of the author into two stages. Yet the
only discernible difference or differences between the essays
before and after 1933 are the result of a process of intellectual
maturation. Stylistically, as the author himself recognized, the
difference between the two periods is evidenced in the author's
increased reliance on his own intuition in examining the problems
mentioned in his essays. The consequence of this increased use
of intuition is that the distance between the writer and the reader
diminishes as the work progresses. The question of unity and
diversity in the works of Picón Salas presents a paradox that lies
at the core of his *errancia*. In rejecting the writings prior to 1933,
the essayist, consciously or unconsciously, provides the reader
with the element of rejection that is necessary to understand in
order to establish the meaning of *errancia* in the author's life.

The author's first departure from Mérida was, in effect, a rejection of the traditions of the past. In time, however, the rejection became nostalgia, and the author felt the need to recreate the memories of youth in *Viaje al amanecer*. Picón Salas, himself, saw the dichotomy between unity and diversity as an essential ingredient in the life of the individual. Life was a series of stages in which biological changes effected the intellectual development of the individual. Notwithstanding the changes, there remains the unity of the personality.

The question of intellectual maturation was a preoccupation evidenced in *Buscando el camino*. For Picón Salas, the transition from adolescence to adulthood represented the acquisition of greater discipline in his writings: "This book, written in my twenties, is iconoclastic, youthful, and without any sense of grammar. There will come a day in which my writing will demonstrate a better understanding of grammar and my paragraphs will be firm and precise, my ideas oriented and joined together with discipline." [5] The underlying need that governed the author's effort to achieve discipline was a desire to establish, as early as possible, his literary identity. In *Buscando el camino* he presented the unity-disunity factor in the physical and intellectual growth of the individual via an imaginary conversation with a wise old man. The dialogue between the author and the old man treats the various ways of perceiving life and the role of the individual in society as he passes through the different stages. The first stage is youth in which physical exuberance parallels the development of ideas: "The decade of one's twenties represents a crazy rebelliousness and an ingenuous enthusiasm." [6] Youth yields, in the middle years of life, to the serenity of mind and body necessary to carry out the responsibilities of developing the country, a home, and the world, ("patria, hogar, y mundo"). Once these responsibilities have been met, the autumn of life brings with it a deserved period of physical and intellectual rest: "In the autumn of one's life it is time to rest. Wearing peasant's sandals it is time to bask in the sun. It is time to behold the ritual of peasant workers sowing the land." [7]

The nature of life as outlined above implies the integration of the different stages. Life itself is seen as a whole. Picón Salas saw the process of maturation extend to the level of historical and cultural development of nation states. Whereas he considered the countries of Europe to be experiencing a stage of intellectual and

cultural maturity, the Latin American countries were seen as
going through the stage of adolescence. He concluded that
Europe, with its vast heritage in the arts, had established its
identity before Latin America had even become independent;
the cultural identity of Spanish American countries, on the other
hand, he said, was still in the process of forming.

The mood generated throughout the essays in *Buscando el
camino* is dominated by a sense of urgency as the author seeks
out the answers to his identity and the relationship of that identity
to Venezuela. From the point of view of the author's life,
Buscando el camino represents the emotional and intellectual
transition from adolescence to young adulthood. The essays offer
a measure of the author's discontent—a sign of the rebelliousness
of youth—with the external reality of his circumstance; they
demonstrate his personal desire to liberate his mind and spirit
from easy accommodation with the status quo in the Andean
province of Mérida and in Venezuela as a whole. The spirit of
adventure, of *errancia*, physically and intellectually, represents
the need for change, a need that develops out of political and
social crisis and the crisis that comes in the transition from youth
to adulthood.

In *Buscando el camino* the reality represented is the historical
trajectory of Venezuela beginning with the days of Bolívar. The
essays contained do not advocate revolution. They are nondog-
matic in their approach to the problems. At most, *Buscando el
camino* is an exhortative collection of essays in which the writer
cries out to other writers of America to search the past for a new
vision of the future. The book is an affirmation of faith both in the
writer's own potential to deal with the myriad problems of
Venezuela and Spanish America and the capacity of his *patria*—
Venezuela and the larger *patria* of Spanish America—in becoming
what it should become. However, what the continent should
become remains undefined. Neither in *Buscando el camino* nor
in subsequent works do we find a prescription for the practical
development of the society. The hope that prevails, on the other
hand, is that some day the Bolivarian dream of political harmony
shall become a reality.

Buscando el camino is a book in search of ideals. Specifically,
for Picón Salas, these ideals were *patria, gloria,* and *amor.* The
pursuit of these ideals was motivated by the author's identification with the spirit and activity of the Venezuelan liberator,

Simón Bolívar. Through the liberal tradition set by Bolívar in his idealistic struggle for Spanish American independence, Picón saw the possibility of discovering a sense of national unity: "Speak of tradition which disappears in the smoke of modernity, tradition which must be conserved in order that [with the passage of generations] *it can give blood to the national soul.*" [8]

Picón Salas' dissatisfaction with the historical past is precisely a disenchantment with the way in which the writers of the past century had projected their image of history. He found particular fault with the deterministic historians, like Laureano Vallenilla Lanz, who provided Venezuela with a fatalistic interpretation of the period of violence in the nineteenth century. Vallenilla Lanz, according to Picón Salas, did not take into consideration the spirit of Venezuela that, compared to the European states, was merely beginning to emerge in the past century: "When a people has lived only for a century, like the mestizo, the nation still has many vestiges of the past which it has not been able to convert into an ethnic sense of individuality. It has not had the opportunity to rest in order to establish a sense of cohesiveness. It has many different climates and different zones, a strip of plains land and a strip of desert, and also a strip of highland. For such a nation, old legal and political formats do not suffice." [9]

Critical of the positivist approach to history, the author was also critical of the exotic and sensualist elements in the literature of Venezuelan modernists. The modernist writers, said Picón, like the positivists, had no comprehension of the true character of the country. In their escapism they, also, inferred a negative and fatalistic interpretation of Venezuela's past. *Buscando el camino,* in a sense, was the essayist's initial attempt to present a contradictory view of the disorder in Venezuelan history: the violence was not an endemic part of the body politic but a matter of circumstance. In affirming the existence of a spiritual essence in Venezuela, he demonstrated the authenticity of a cultural and æsthetic reality yet to be revealed. The essayist saw in the modernist's elitism an evasionary tactic to avoid confrontation with his environment; Picón Salas stated the necessity to meet the problems of national disunity and attempt to resolve them. In a later essay, Picón defined the purpose of his pursuit of the intellectual heritage of Venezuela as follows: "Against empiricism, violence, the unexpected and the adventurism of the creole, we ought to invoke the use of intelligence which knows how to plan things. Intelligence, not as a mere adornment or useful object for evading problems, but for understanding and revealing to us the facts about our land." [10] The purpose of searching for the *inteligencia venezolana* was to reconstruct the course of history in terms of a spiritual progress leading toward political and intellectual freedom: "It is a kind of plan in order to recover time, the time which Bolívar accelerated and which later was pushed backward during the dark period of our ignorance and our laziness." [11]

In *Buscando el camino,* Picón Salas began to develop a neoclassical vision of progress in Venezuelan history. He held to the idea that men could, through the exercise of will, determine the course of the future. Men had the power to create their country (*hacer patria*); they were not subject to the vicissitudes of historical events. Since, for the essayist, history was subordinate to literature, he thought that the moral responsibility for reconstructing the country rested in the hands of men of letters. In *Buscando el camino,* he charged the writers of America to participate in the historical process by combining their art with the destiny of the country: "Make the work of art, a work of ideas with a particular American interest. You will be able to do it better than others because you have seen it with your own eyes. You will, thus, complete the work of an old hero who lived in modern times. His name was Simón Bolívar. He knew these skies, he walked this land, and he formed this country. But the work of Simón Bolívar never ends." [12]

III   *The Sense of* Patria

Venezuela insinuates herself in the first collection of essays as a source of spiritual and emotional inspiration for the author. The nation is perceived through the personage of Bolívar, the grandfathers of the author, the writers José Gil Fortoul and Laureano Vallenilla Lanz, and the lyrical description of the flora of the province of Mérida. Venezuela is the nucleus of the writer's commitment to his art. The *patria* is the goal toward which, as far as Picón Salas is concerned, all men of conscience in the country should aspire: "The spiritual multiplicity of Bolívar, the spear of Paez, Boves falling upon defenseless cities like a messenger of death, the superhuman daring feats of Las

Queseras, Bolívar dying in exile like a Greek hero, comprise the
poetic flame which consumes all of us. Later there were new
wars, new internecine struggles, new poetic motives." [13]

Patria is both an ethical and aesthetic concept in the essays.
In the phrase "formar patria" ("to form the country"), there is
evident a sense of obligation for the writer in America to participate in this monumental task. The task itself should be ap-
proached as if it were a vocation: "The task of the Latin American
writer must be one similar to that of an apostle." [14] For the
author, the individual in society has no other choice but to
accept and carry out this responsibility. To do otherwise is to
deny the existence of a part of self. Consequently, when Picón
Salas speaks of the integrity of the individual, he is referring to a
relationship between internal, or personal reality, and the external one formed by the traditions and institutions that exist in
the country. The individual must find a way to incorporate his
life into the life of the country. Picón recognized that coming to
terms with the external reality of the country is in a sense an act
of accommodation. He did not see it, however, as an accommodation with a particular political system; the accommodation is
with the very existence of the country as a fundamental reality.

The country in which the individual is born provides the mold
of external form and offers certain ethical guidelines for individual action. To internalize that form is in itself a form of
liberation from chaos. Furthermore, only by accepting the
responsibilities of forming the country does a "country" become
the affective entity known as *patria*. The discovery of this in-
timacy between the individual and *patria* results in an aesthetic
fruition of harmony between the reality within and the reality
without. The concept of *patria*, as we have seen, combining
aesthetic and ethical elements, forges a union between liberation
and creation, between form and content. The problem in Latin
America, as Picón Salas saw it, was that the form of the continent
had not yet been decided. There did not exist a harmony between
the individual and *patria*: "The projects of Bolívar have yet to
be accomplished. The road to freedom has not been finished.
This does not mean that we must recreate Carabobos and
Ayacuchos. With verses similar to those we sing to our sweet-
hearts and to our friends, we can contribute to the completion of
these projects by putting into our poetry and into our prose the

feeling, the countryside, and the men of our country. In this way we forge the development of our country. In this way we can liberate it." [15]

The act of liberation that begins in *Buscando el camino* and culminates in *Comprensión de Venezuela* is manifested in two ways: first, the denial of the historical inevitability of the violence and the dictatorships of the nineteenth and twentieth centuries, and second, by the increase in Venezuela's awareness of its own cultural heritage. As in *Literatura venezolana*, Picón Salas saw in Venezuela a particular form of the cultural unity of Spanish America and Western civilization. It is important to note in the development of the concept of *patria* the effort to extend the meaning of the word to the larger cultural entity of Spanish America. In *Buscando el camino* there exists, at first, only a hint of this development. Later on in life, when the author gets ready to leave his homeland, the conceptualization of the thought of a larger homeland (*patria grande*) becomes more clearly defined: "If for a brief period of time I lost contact with my country, there rose up in my awareness of life the color and the enigma of a larger homeland similar to the one which Bolívar, with his Venezuelan plainsmen, went in search of as he passed through the forests, over the highlands of this Continent, across rivers and over the humps of the cordilleras until he arrived in Cuzco, the land of the sun." [16] The identification of the idea of *patria* is relative to the trajectory of the author's *errancia*. In Mérida, *patria* is the Andean province; in Caracas, *patria* will be Venezuela; in Chile and Mexico, *patria* becomes Spanish America. When the author eventually travels to Europe for the first time in 1937 as chargé d'affairs in Prague, he sees himself representing the whole of Latin America; he considers the nucleus of self as South American. Then, after having visited and traveled throughout Europe, it becomes implicit, as in *Los malos salvajes,* that he has acquired another citizenship in the world of Western culture. The concept of *patria,* seen in its extension in the concept *patria grande,* is the emotive element in the intellectual voyage that takes him from provincial life to the world beyond the confines of Venezuela.

For Picón Salas, the *patria chica* of his existence was the Andean village of Mérida, located in the western portion of Venezuela near the frontier separating the country from Colombia. In the early works, *Buscando el camino, Mundo imaginario,*

and *Odisea de tierra firme,* Mérida or *patria chica* represents
the narrow limits of human experience. Mérida is a vision of life
prior to the author's peregrination. It is also life in an idyllic
state represented by a love affair with a farmer's daughter, the
aroma of orange groves and coffee plantations, and an image of
the diaphanous waters of her mountain streams. In the essays
Mérida provides the source for the expression of his lyricism.
From the point of view of voyage, Mérida in *Buscando el camino*
comes to represent the point of departure. In *Viaje al amanecer,*
the Andean province represents a return to a paradise lost. Both
as a point of departure and of return, Mérida produced a conflict between emotion and intellect in Picón Salas.

In *Buscando el camino,* the Andean province is seen in a
reference to orchids or in a description of an idyllic pastoral
setting: "The sight of peasant girls, tanned the color of mahogany,
peasant girls received by the sun, while you gather up the grains
in fields of coffee, while you ride young colts with your lasso
after unwilling calfs. In the meantime the rustic sun which hangs
over the plowed fields tinges your cheeks with the color of this
tropical land." [17] In this description the sensuality of the setting
is tempered by the introduction of the ethical theme of conduct.
The resulting juxtaposition is between the purity and sincerity of
life in the province as compared to the temptations of the city.

Mérida, hidden in a valley of the Andean mountains, becomes,
for Picón Salas, a second symbol of the resolution of the internal
strife in Venezuela. Of all the cities in the nineteenth century,
Mérida seems to have suffered least from the ravages of the
Federalist Wars. In Mérida both Federalist and anti-Federalist
appear to have discovered a neutral ground. Picón points out in
an essay dealing with his grandfathers, that one was a conservative and the other a liberal. In the temperate climate of Mérida,
they resolved their differences: "In the middle of the crazy
disorder of my room the photographs of my two grandparents
face one another, one thin and the other rosy cheeked." [18]

CHAPTER 4

Errancia: *A Spiritual Becoming and an Intellectual Awakening*

I *A Spiritual Becoming*

THE voyage of *errancia* toward the discovery of a cultural and spiritual identity is a process in which both the individual and the country become more and more like the aesthetic-ethical ideal that inspired the odyssey. In *Comprensión de Venezuela*, as we shall see in Chapter 6, this formational process is referred to by Picón Salas as the process of *devenir* ("a becoming"). In terms of Venezuelan culture and society the implication by Picón Salas is that the country had not brought to fruition its full potential; the conditions of life were not what they ought to have been. *Devenir* is a concept referring to the cultural process leading toward social and political utopia. It is a dynamic concept. While the utopia of a perfect society may never be reached, the movement toward the formation of a more felicitous reality never ceases. The concept of becoming is one of spiritual and cultural growth; it applies also to the intellectual growth of the individual in society. *Devenir* is the process of renovation occurring at each instant in historical time through the assimilation of new and different cultural forms.

Culturally speaking *devenir* in the Latin American context is synonymous with the development of a creole or mestizo society. For Picón Salas, the concept of a mestizo culture, the result of *devenir*, transcended the consideration of the word "mestizo" as a genetic factor. It signified a process of cultural elaboration and changing forms. Picón paralleled the evolution of Latin American culture with the development of Greek culture, the original prototype for the spiritual process of *devenir:* "Greek style takes on a vital process of elaboration. It is not the result of

62

a material law but a process of becoming."[1] Latin America's mestizo society represented the continuation of the process of becoming in a universal and historical continuum.

In applying the term *devenir* to the reality of Venezuelan circumstance, Picón Salas was influenced by the dialectical approach to history found in Hegel. The difference between Picón Salas and Hegel is that Hegel was more theoretical. In Picón Salas we discover, as shall be demonstrated, an intuitive and practical application of Hegelian thesis, antithesis, and synthesis.

The Hegelian search for utopia provides for an understanding of history as an ascent toward perfection.[2] The movement of history is from a lower order of truth to a higher and more absolute form, with the search culminating in the acquisition of absolute or universal truth. Each step of the way, as each historical phase, is only a part of the whole truth. Alone, no phase represents the whole, just as for Picón Salas no single period of Venezuelan history represented the whole of the country's historical-cultural development. In Hegel, the historical trajectory toward truth was based on the concept of the universal law of rhythmic change; Picón Salas saw the process of change as a natural phenomenon. Hegel structured his concept of becoming in terms of the confrontation between thesis and antithesis. This confrontation produced a new synthesis which Hegel saw as developing into a new thesis to be met by an approaching new antithesis. For Picón Salas, the struggle between thesis and antithesis in Latin American history began with the confrontation between the Spanish *conquistadores* and the indigenous cultures; the resulting synthesis was the mestizo culture which achieved its political independence in the nineteenth century. Hegel's concept of the progressive movement of history was an idealist theory in search of eternal values; in Picón Salas the search for a new cultural synthesis was also idealistic to the extent that he saw the process as continuous.

Karl Marx, in the nineteenth century, attempted to limit the progressive concepts of Hegel by suggesting that the search for utopia would culminate in the dictatorship of the proletariat. At about the time of the Russian Revolution in 1917, the Marxian search for the practial solution to the historical conflict between social classes began to infiltrate the intellectual circles of Latin America. Picón Salas, like the socialists, was also concerned with improving the conditions of life. The difference in approach toward the problems of the contintent between the Marxist theorists and Picón Salas was twofold: first, he remained closer to the original concepts of Hegel in the pursuit of eternal spiritual and cultural values, and second, the concept of *errancia* coupled with *devenir* prohibited the essayist from accepting any dogmatic approach to history. Existence, he said, was too complex to admit of any theory of life which had the effect of limiting the experiences of man and society. Life and Latin America, for Picón Salas, were mysteries that had to be resolved through intuition as well as science: "Life conserved for me all its magical mystery. Through a poem or through the music of my own dream world, I searched for the other shoreline of the incomprehensible and the unexplainable, of all that which lies beyond mere factual existence."[3]

The peregrination, or *errancia*, in pursuit of essence, truth, and utopia is endless. It is, as stated by Siso Martínez, *inacabado* ("unfinished").[4] The ideals of the writer constantly move him to transform exterior reality. Utopia is perceived only as a potential reality, but as a potential reality it becomes the reality of the author's intellectual peregrination. Herein, there is evident in the search for utopia a form of romantic irony. While the state of perfection can only be imagined and hoped for in terms of its becoming a tangible reality, the search for perfection comes to be the fundamental reality of the author's writings.

The concept of the *criollo*, or mestizo, in Latin America represents, in the work of Picón Salas, an historical union, or synthesis, between the conquerors and the conquered. The cultural concept of the *criollo*, in Picón Salas, is less concrete than the genetic interpretation offered by José Vasconcelos in *La raza cósmica* (*The Cosmic Race*). Where Vasconcelos attempted to present an almost Darwinian view of the evolution of Latin America, Picón Salas saw the process of creolization as part of the cultural and historical development of Western civilization. The *criollo* as a sociocultural reality, in Picón Salas, exemplifies a process of intellectual and cultural diffusion and assimilation leading toward the creation of a new and more perfect civilization.

Similar to the cultural process, the search for self-realization constantly remains an unfinished and interminable task. As man develops physically so does the spiritual element of self.

However, the spiritual essence of man, according to Picón Salas, can only achieve its full vitality by becoming as it should. The paradox, here, and as we discover in Hegel, is that the physical self often inhibits the development of the spirit. Yet, without the physical world, the spirit would not discover in the cultural heritage and in the geography of the land the values that permit it to thrive. For Picón Salas, reality consisted of both internal and external reality. In developing his ideas about personal and national identity, he attempted to harmonize the conflict between internal and external reality, between the effects of the mind and of the body.

While Picón Salas was particularly concerned with the discovery of the spiritual identity of Venezuela, the ultimate goal of that discovery was to project a vision of the identity of mankind in the pursuit of spiritual and cultural progress. The collection of essays, *Los malos salvajes,* is a book dealing with just such universal considerations. In the final essay Picón Salas examines the search for utopia, the omega of Teilhard de Chardin. De Chardin's belief in the evolutionary progress of mankind toward a more perfect society coincided with Picon's own views of history. In the last paragraph he urged the universal acceptance of Chardin's philosophy; he interpreted this philosophy as a challenge to the negativism of the twentieth century. The process of *devenir* in Picón Salas is, in reality, a process that extends from self, to nation, to continent, to Western civilization, to mankind in general.

Specifically, Picón Salas applied his interpretation of the process of becoming to the struggle for self-realization in Venezuela and in Latin America. The essayist saw the struggle in the historiography of Venezuela as one between pessimists like Augusto Mijares, who interpreted the violence and the institution of *caudillismo* of the nineteenth century as part of the organic structure of society, and optimists such as himself, who viewed the events of history as controllable through the will of men. The future, he said, must be written by men who see the progressive movement of history as the result of organization and intention. The past must not be interpreted as a mere adventure, but must serve as a lesson for what is to become:

We oppose events produced by chance, the surprises of yesterday, the notion of history as an adventure, with a new sense of history, one which is the result of plans and organized through our will. Our purpose is to make the nature of the creole sense of equality for which the Venezuelan struggled and bled for more than a century the moral basis of our history. This is what I would call the Venezuelan thesis, the positive result which we have to consciously make strong after the tremendous trial which our past life represents.[6]

Picón sought only to provide an attitude toward change. In his view, history was an extension of individual life, and he intuited the capacity of men to reverse the course of history through the exercise of their intellect and free will. On the level of the individual the forces of nature were represented in human passion. The contest, then, between civilization and nature can be seen in Picón Salas as one between intelligence or spirit, and passion. The answer to the problem of history had to be found in the union and harmonious relationship between these two elements. It would not be found in the suppression of passion by intellect. Such a reversal of power would only produce a new form of tyranny, a *despotismo ilustrado* ("an intellectually informed despotism"). He discovered the answer to the question of harmony in the figure of Santos Luzardo, the protagonist of Romulo Gallegos' novel, *Doña Bárbara*. Santos Luzardo represented the synthesis between spirit and nature not because he defeated Doña Bárbara, but because he learned how to come to terms with the wilderness of Venezuela through the process of domestication. At the end of the novel Santos Luzardo did not retreat from the difficulties inherent in attempting to domesticate the region of the *llanos*. Luzardo symbolized an opposition to the modernist retreat from the problems of Venezuela's hinterland to the cultured salons of urban life. He comprehended the forces of nature and saw the possibilities in turning wilderness into productive land: "The formula of America, within the old and conflicting problem already studied by Sarmiento in *Facundo* was not so much that the cult of Santos Luzardo, with his university title and advocating a pretentious way of life, would become an exclusive and absorbing way of life for the plainsman— the formula of all those who have called themselves enlightened despots—but that this cult would be useful in better understanding and in improving the vital experience of life." [7]

The process of becoming in Picón Salas, either for the individual or the nation, contains within it a moral imperative. It presupposes a dissatisfaction with self or the status quo and the need to become not what one is or has been but what one ought to be. In terms of the individual it is a formation from within. The same principle can be applied with regard to the nation. The past does not have a deterministic value in Picón's vision of the future; it is important to understand it, however, in order to be aware of the underlying forces that have produced the particular identity of Venezuela. The process of becoming in the trajectory of *errancia* extends from within to without. Life is viewed in terms of a progression that leads the individual, or Venezuela, from the known to the unknown, from a particular reality to a more universal one. Becoming is also a kind of dismantling of the stereotypes that perpetuate themselves in the traditions of the people. These have the effect of restricting the movement and growth of the society. In the process of becoming, a particular vision of life is confronted with a larger one. Beyond the boundaries of rural life in Mérida lay the life-style of the *llanos*, and beyond the wilderness the structure of urban existence. Beyond Venezuela were the other countries of Latin America and beyond that the European citadel of Western civilization. For Picón Salas, *errancia* as a pilgrimage is an awakening to these realities beyond Venezuela. As one stereotype falls, a new and larger one takes its place. The process of becoming is the process of an expansion of one's vision of the world.

II   *An Intellectual Awakening*

It is apparent that *errancia* has both a physical and spiritual dimension in the work of Picón Salas. In *Mundo imaginario* it is the writer himself who crosses the Venezuelan frontier in pursuit of new concepts of life and new ways of experiencing reality. The reminiscences contained in *Mundo imaginario* project outwardly as the writer explains his emergence from a world of dreams and a limited vision of reality. It represents the formation of his personal identity as he awakens to the circumstances of the outside world.

The emergence from dreams to a larger reality is symbolized in the anecdotal narrative entitled *Los fantasmas de la infancia: El inglés (The Ghosts of Our Youth: The Englishman)*. Picón Salas recollects that as a child the order and tranquillity of his household was maintained, at least as far as the children were concerned, through the legend of the English corsair, who was said to reside in his mother's pantry. Legend had it that the spirit of the corsair would emerge at night to steal recalcitrant children away from their homes, send them off to England in a pirate ship, and have their bodies turned into a tender shank of ham or a foie gras. The legend, according to Picón Salas, had its genesis in the colonial period when, in truth, English pirates did ravage the coastal cities of Venezuela and eventually made their way inland to the valley of Mérida. Even though the age of piracy had disappeared, as far as the children were concerned the spirit of the evil Englishman structured their lives in presenting to them certain limitations to their freedom to move and act. The pantry, where their mother kept all the sweet delicacies, represented the threshold between the known and the unknown. Only an act of great courage would have permitted them to open the door and discover the nonexistence of the Englishman. As stated by the author, in the mind of the children their destiny lay in the very phlegm of the Englishman. But the passage from childhood to adolescence and then to young adulthood is precisely, in the concept of Picón Salas, the process of the dissipation of fears of the unknown. All that is required is the cultivation of some degree of skepticism and daring. So it was that one day an older cousin, Paquito, visited Picón Salas' home. After several hours of play the children, exhausted and hungry, decided to see what was in the pantry. Notwithstanding the warning of the young Picón, Paquito broke the lock and opened the pantry door. Not only did the children satisfy their hunger but they succeeded in destroying the legend of the Englishman. "We had discarded a myth of our youth and given a mortal blow to the power of England." [8]

The significance of Paquito's audacity in defying the warning of the legend was to expand the limitations of reality. For the first time the children were made aware that a given perception of reality is only valid in terms of the conditions in which that reality is viewed. Once the conditions change, in this case the passage from childhood to adolescence, reality must be reinterpreted and redefined.

The Venezuelan experience Picón Salas described in *Odisea de tierra firme* parallels the experience of the children alluded to in *Mundo imaginario*. In the political, social, and economic life of the nineteenth century, particularly after the Wars of Federation, the limitations of political and social realities were defined through the stereotype of *caudillismo*. Until the rise to power of Antonio Guzmán Blanco, the country was fragmented into territories controlled by local strong men or caudillos. In each region order was maintained through coercion and physical force. Each caudillo projected an image of invincibility and immersed that image in the fears and legends of the local populace with the aid of a witch doctor, or *adivino*.

In the chapter, "Tiempos federales" ("The Federalist Period"), Picón provides us with a prototype of this kind of caudillo in the figure of Martín Espinoza. Espinoza controlled the region known as Portuguesa, which was populated by blacks, mulattoes, and Indians. In the political and social upheaval that followed the overthrow of General José Tadeo Monagas, Espinoza rallied about him the inhabitants of the *llanos* and polarized the struggle between nonwhites and whites to suit his own drive for power: "Boys, we have to rise up against the whites. They had unseated General Monagas in order to return us to slavery. They even want to sell us to the English for them to make our flesh into soap and to make us Christians." [9] Espinoza's second in command was a witch doctor, el Adivino de Guanarito, who reigned over the spiritual world of Portuguesa. When Espinoza spoke to the people in the village square, the Adivino was always by his side. In his attire and mannerisms, el Adivino symbolized the supernatural forces of the underworld that determined the limits of the people's intellectual awareness of the world: "A strange and wild man. He doesn't even speak to his people. He is a representative of the supernatural world. He appears as a crusader brandishing a black cross in his hand. He walks hunched over and the rug he wears accentuates his monstrous priesthood. His yellow eyes, like that of a cameleon, render powerless those who are unhappy. He imposes silence and creates a fear which sews up people's mouths." [10] Through the indecipherable and mysterious incantations of the Adivino, the caudillo was able to absorb the will of the people and command them to do his bidding.

In comparing the anecdote of the pantry with that of the caudillo Martín Espinoza, there surfaces an underlying message which combines personal experience with historical experience. Both life and history in order to remain vital must integrate the past with a sense of change leading toward the future. The present, for Picón Salas, represented a threshold, as was the door of the pantry, between the known and the unknown. The present represented the active dimension in life. The action that Picón Salas called for in both accounts was the process of demythologizing the past. The nature of temporal synthesis in which past and present create the future and the dialectical conflict in the process of *devenir* is one of converting old myths into new stereotypes, or realities.

We have already alluded to Picón Salas' affection for the *pícaro* ("rogue") in Spanish literature. In *Buscando el camino* the essayist viewed the work of Fernando de Rojas as challenging the religious obscurantism of medieval society. Picón Salas' concern was not so much with the *pícaro's* relationship to the cosmology of orthodox Catholicism nor to the particular religious doctrine. What Picón criticized was the institutional obscurantism of Catholic Spain in its attempt to codify the behavior of man, stripping him of the possibility of expressing, in any spontaneous way, the spirit of his individuality. The *pícaro* in the work of Picón represents, in a sense, the adventurism inherent in the meaning of *errancia* as a peregination and a search for few forms of physical reality. For Picón Salas the errancy of the *pícaro* expressed the desire to experience life, to extend the limitations of reality beyond traditionalism and the requisites of the status quo. As he stated in the essay "El año 1920" ("The Year 1920"), "Beyond our mountains and domestic tyrannies the world was changing terribly, and we wanted to get close in order to see its face. We wanted to be men of our time; we wanted to drown ourselves in it and no longer remain anxious witnesses of a sleepy province." [11]

In the milieu of Mérida, Picón Salas experienced a way of life that suppressed the expression of individual freedom. He interpreted the control that the church had over people's lives as obscurantist in nature. His quarrel was not, however, with religion itself, but with the church as an institution. According to the essayist, the church, since colonial times, had erred in aligning itself with the *encomenderos* ("colonial land holders") and had become an instrument of repression. It had evolved as a ceremonial church that had substituted for the evangelizing spirit and message of love brought to America by the first missionaries, like Bartolomé de las Casas, the trappings of formula and ceremony. But worst of all for Picón Salas, the teachers of religion had stripped the people of their capacity to use their free will. They threatened the people by warning them of the fires of hell should they express the needs of human passion.

Picón Salas needed to participate in the tangible forms of life that existed beyond Mérida and Venezuela. The placidity and routine of life in Mérida could not satisfy his thirst for adventure. In terms of the traditional struggle between Cain and Abel in the world, Picón equates his situation with that of the former: "Cain no longer thinks that his is a terrestrial Paradise. He thinks that beyond the small limits where his tent made of animal skin is set up, and where each sheep has its own name, and where the sun extends itself over what he has inherited from his father there awaits a more brilliant world, which may be unedited and perhaps monstrous and which may be a world of guilt and evil, yet it may be a world he can make into his own likeness and image (as if he could challenge God.)" [12]

The intellectual flight from control over the expression of free will is first identified in the the essay *La fuga de Carlos* (*The flight of Carlos*). The figure of Carlos, who was a classmate of the author in the seminary school in Mérida, represents, in his skepticism, an intellectual rogue who challenges the religious truths of Padre Quiroz, the Jesuit teacher of religion and catechism. Similar to Paquito, Carlos succeeded in trespassing beyond the limits of what is known. Until the moment of Carlos' challenge the students had been mesmerized by the priest's ability to rationalize all philosophical problems in terms of the eternal truths present in Catholic dogma. As Picón Salas states in the essay, "His was a philosophy capable of convincing the most hardened heretics, and because of his capacity to reason and to create syllogisms which shot forth like arrows we sustained the arguments of Padre Quiroz." [13] One day Carlos received a controversial book, *Conflictos entre la religión y la ciencia* (*Conflicts Between Religion and Science*) which argued the incompatibility between science and religion. It presented the positivist thesis that religion would eventually disappear. When he posited the thesis in class, he drew nothing but silence from Padre Quiroz: "Father Quiroz himself stopped short in the middle of the argument he was unraveling." [14] The Jesuit was unprepared for the theories of scientific positivism. The only doubts that he knew how to handle were traditional. What Carlos suggested in class was a whole new way of looking at reality, a new way of establishing the relationship between man, his work, and the universe. Beyond Mérida the world was changing. Through the use of scientific methodology, man seemed to be harnessing the forces of nature, controlling them for his own

purposes. Technology was developing for man a new cosmology:
"After every mechanical invention, every improvement in photog-
raphy and in the movies, the development of the telephone, wars,
and airplane flights, there have sprung forth new ways to live and
feel life." [15]

Somehow the students in the class through their intuition understood the merit of Carlos' arguments. Padre Quiroz lost the battle.
The reaction of the class was one of quiet satisfaction. The young
students awakened to a less defined and more linear vision of
reality. Truth became relative. Carlos gave to his classmates a view
of the potential of human activity liberated from the limits of
Padre Quiroz' aprioristic view of life and the function of men in
society. Carlos, in the essay by Picón Salas, represents the incarnation of the spirit of intellectual *errancia* which drew the students
from the center of their existence to the world beyond the mountains of Mérida.

CHAPTER 5

An Intellectual Voyage

I *Caracas 1920*

IN 1920, Picón Salas left the Andean province of Mérida for the first time on a journey that would, three years later, take him to Chile. At nineteen he had grown restless in the serenity and security of provincial life. Beyond the mountains of Mérida, he thought, lay the challenges of a changing world that would satisfy his intellectual curiosity and spirit of adventure. Mérida, on the other hand, had the appearance, as he was to say in *Mundo imaginario*, of a region lost in the memory of its traditions and routine. The trip to Caracas on board the steamer *El Progreso* was a voyage of *errancia* to meet the challenge of new realities; it was a trip to find a new order of life. Symbolically, the trip of Picón Salas from the known to the unknown typified a journey of an entire generation of intellectuals in Mérida who, filled with hope and national ideals, sought to discover their identity and to establish in the historiography of Venezuela a route similar to Don Quixote's: "On the road—like the road of the young Don Quixote— I will find inns and inn-keepers, young girls and servants, new countrysides with differing climates, other students who yielded to the same temptations and moved to Caracas. Caracas was only the first name, the first step along the road of our perplexed minds." [1]

The Caracas that Picón Salas encountered in 1920 was quickly moving into the technological and industrial age. Six years prior to the essayist's arrival in the capital, the first oil well was discovered in Lake Maracaibo by a subsidiary of the Royal-Dutch-Shell Corporation. By 1917, over half a billion barrels of petroleum had been extracted from the bottom of the lake. As interest in the natural resources of Venezuela increased, Caracas became populated with immigrants from all over the world, and by 1920 had

73

74   MARIANO PICÓN SALAS

become one of the more cosmopolitan cities in Latin America. The
migration to the city from without was complemented by a steady
stream of farmers and ranchers (*llaneros*) from the interior sections
of the country who sought to take advantage of the economic boom.
A small middle class of merchants was created, and by 1930
Venezuela was the only country in the hemisphere able to pay
off its foreign and domestic debt. Economically, the country was
progressing and moving from a traditional and monocultural rural
society to a modern state.[2]

Politically, the reverse was true. Venezuela was still living the
legacy of *caudillismo* that had begun to develop as a political institution shortly after the Wars of Independence. In 1908, Juan
Vicente Gómez overthrew the previous caudillo, Cipriano Castro,
to become one of the most ruthless leaders in Venezuelan history.[3]
The Caracas that Picón Salas discovered in 1920 was still dominated by the power of Gómez. Notwithstanding the dictator's
associations with representatives of the international oil companies
and their investors, Gómez conducted the affairs of state with the
mentality of a feudal lord. His attitude toward the country and
its people was that of the traditional *padrino* ("godfather"), who
felt that all he surveyed was his personal property and that the
people of the country should be grateful for his leadership. Under
Gómez, law and order was maintained at the sole discretion of
the dictator. He gathered about him intellectuals and investors
who rationalized his absolute control of the country as essential
for a nation whose political past had been so chaotic. One such
intellectual was Laureano Vallenilla Lanz. In his book *Cesarismo
democrático*, Vallenilla Lanz attempted to prove the democratic
character of Caesar—Gómez—in representing the will and desire
of a people consciously, or unconsciously, in search of a paternalistic leader.[4]

In the political and intellectual atmosphere created by Gómez,
the young Picón Salas did not find the utopia of his dreams. He,
along with other young intellectuals, encountered only disappointment in their first confrontation with the reality of the city.
In spite of the wealth of the country, due to the production of oil,
the majority of the people were poor, living on the fringes of survival. Only those who actively supported the caudillo lived com-
fortably. Since his power was absolute, when the people needed
something to be done they had no choice but to make their request directly to the dictator. And in return for the favor, Gómez

was awarded the title of El Benemérito (the Worthy One). When in later life Picón Salas wrote his intellectual autobiography *Regreso de tres mundos*, he described the chagrin and disillusionment felt upon arriving in Caracas: "Caracas in 1920, more than the capital of the republic, seemed to represent a Venezuelan deception. Was this the city I wondered about? I said to myself as I descended from the station to confront the long line of proletarian huts perched along the cliff. I heard people shouting and screaming in a way which startled me on account of my polite upbringing in the province. I heard a manner of address which we did not distinguish as either cordial or insolent. . . ." [5]

The influence of his grandfather, whose liberal philosophy toward religion and politics Picón Salas learned at an early age, aided in developing in the author a natural skepticism toward any form of absolutism. [6] In Caracas, however, he discovered another form of oppression, which he had not anticipated. Gómez, through a system of paid informers, had suppressed freedom of expression; the price for dissidence was immediate imprisonment. Instead of a vibrant cultural life the intellectuals of the Generation of 1920 were confronted with an air of despondency and intellectual impotency. As the essayist was to say, life in Caracas seemed comparable to living in a pool of stagnant water: "A stagnant pool of black and still waters, where the only thing heard is the croaking of frogs . . ." (*E*, 1375).

Perplexed by what they found in the capital, the young intellectuals sought in vain for answers to the dichotomy between the spiritual inertia of the present and the spirit of independence and freedom symbolized in their national hero, Simón Bólivar. In the Plaza Bolívar they gathered to find reasonable answers to their questions from the writers and intellectuals of an older generation. One theory that prevailed stated that Bolívar himself was responsible for creating the institution of *caudillismo* and the period of violence it brought to the country. It was said that the liberator, when he crossed into Colombia to eliminate the Spanish domination of the continent, took with him the best of Venezuelan manhood to fight the Spaniards. After the victory at Ayacucho, the only warriors to return to Venezuela were those suffering from battle fatigue; the more valiant had died in the Wars of Liberation. [7] It was further stated that during the struggle for independence, Caracus had suffered greatly by losing a significant portion of the more educated members of the society. A power

vacuum was created, and the only men left to govern the country
were the opportunistic and illiterate ranchers from the plains
region. It was suggested that perhaps the course of history would
be eventually redirected. In the meantime, Venezuela needed a
strong leader in order for the country to develop a sense of national unity.

For Picón Salas, such an interpretation of Venezuela's past and
present was meaningless and counterproductive. It represented
nothing less than an accommodation with the dictator Gómez; it
was, further, the rationalization of men who in their frustration
with the political situation had lost their ideals. Caracas, as the
author remembered, was suffering a spiritual lethargy, which he
compared to the oppressiveness of Venezuela's tropical sun:
"Above the sky of Caracas there hangs a noonday sun, hot and
motionless. One of those overpious women sneaks out along the
white wall of the church. The trees of the plaza shake their tops
like someone filled with sleep. A heavy streetcar creaks along
over the rails and the asphalt. In the distance can be heard the
bugle call from a barracks" (E, 1377).

Like the idealistic Don Quixote, the Generation of 1920 had
come to Caracas to defeat the monsters of Venezuela's past and to
impose on the nation an enlightened form of justice ("vencer
monstruos e imponer la justicia") (E, 1372). They also thought
they would find in the expression of their sensitivities to life a new
source for their creativity. Their ideals shattered, Caracas came to
represent the harsh reality of the society of men. Life in Caracas
signified the loss of innocence: "Every pure soul who entered the
city in which only the more daring and cynical triumphed had to
ask himself if it was worth the effort to seek out, like Parsifal in
search of the holy grail, their idealism. How many generations
have felt frustrated pursuing that divine cup of freedom, freedom
which is necessary to produce a happy people" (E, 1369). They
saw represented in the brothels of Caracas the grotesqueness and
artificiality of life in the macrocosm of the city: "We passed by the
grotesque details of the house. We heard the harsh voice of a
Celestina-like figure, witnessed the gesticulations of the homo-
sexual muscian playing the piano, saw the tough clients—perhaps
members of the police force—getting drunk, wiffed the cheap
aroma of perfume, anis, and the starched bedclothes of the house.
And also with shame we passed through the galleries with their

multicolored windows where a young girl invited us to her room"
(*E*, 1373).

In the Caracas of 1920, Picón Salas interpreted that men had
not yet learned to sublimate their passions in the pursuit of culture.
For the author, Caracas presented a picture of the dehumanization of society through the immorality of its leaders: "Cows, like
women, have their cycle for giving birth. The cow bellows to the
one who dries out her udders and gives herself over to the butch-
er's knife. And the prisoner's bedsores indicate when it is time to
free him, to send him to the infirmary or to search for a casket.
Nature continues to make the rivers grow. It lifts up clouds of
dust and raises to the heavens the wild sounds of beasts. It makes
the jaguar howl and the serpent hiss in the fields of Venezuela"
(*E*, 1370).

II   *The Venezuelan Exodus of 1923*

The frustration and disenchantment with life in the capital
precipitated, in the Generation of 1920, the need to leave the
country in search of their personal identity. Revolution was an
impossibility. There were no dissident groups powerful enough
to depose the dictator. Gómez had effectively minimized all opposition to his authority. In 1923 the dictatorship became even
more oppressive. A strike by streetcar conductors gave the caudillo
the rationale for imposing martial law on the country; the police
force, which owed its allegiance to no one but Gómez, went from
boardinghouse to boardinghouse rounding up all students sus-
pected of participating or helping the strikers. No sooner were
some students rounded up and carted off to prison, than others,
broken in mind and body were released as a reminder of Gómez'
wrath. As indicated by Picón Salas, the tactics of the police in
carrying out Gómez' orders achieved the desired effect: "Those
ex-prisoners returning from the dictator's dungeons always filled
me with fear. With their bones and hormones undone, they walked
through the street like ghosts, as if they were attempting to avoid
invisible jailers." [8]

For Picón Salas, the threatening political situation that developed in the city presented a moral dilemma. Was it better to con-
serve life by leaving the country in the hope that some day the
dictator would be gone? Or, did it demonstrate a higher moral

principal to sacrifice oneself in political action by opposing the
dictator? On the other hand, individual action would, at best, only
achieve a temporary martyrdom. Gómez was too powerful. The
only logical solution was to leave Venezuela as had other generations of intellectuals who could not accommodate themselves to
the prevailing dictatorship. If the country could not be saved, then
at least, felt Picón, he had the obligation to protect himself. Furthermore, Picón Salas and the others of his generation were
determined to discover the rest of the continent, where, in opposition to the static life in Caracas, reforms were taking place
that might eventually bring about the Bolivarian dream of Pan-
Americanism. Influenced by Alberto Adriani, one of their own
generation, the young intellectuals conceived a plan for the future
deposal of the dictator.[9] They would reeducate themselves in experiencing the reality of life in other countries; they would develop
a new intellectual synthesis for resolving the conflict between
man and his environment; they would then reintegrate themselves with the reality of life in Venezuela and upon return to the
country would procede to restructure the educational system. In
1923, as Picón Salas wrote, "The Venezuelan exodus began in
those years which coincided with the dictatorship. Many of us
left, almost secretly, to suffer, to remake ourselves in foreign
lands" (D, 1378). The history of Venezuela in 1923 once again became divided between the internal conditions that perpetuated
the power of the dictator and the situation of the exiles pursuing
their elusive goals of reform outside the country.[10]

III   Chile: 1923–1936

Before leaving Venezuela for Chile, Mariano Picón Salas returned, briefly, to the Mérida of his youth to discover another
source of disappointment: the economic ruin of his family. His
father had owned a coffee plantation near the foothills of the
Andes. Several months prior to the author's return, the international price of the commodity began to fall, making it impossible
for the father to meet his obligations with his creditors. It became
necessary to auction off the land. And for Picón Salas it appeared
that the essence of his own identity was being sold on the auction
block. Leaving Mérida in 1920 was an intellectual journey; his
return, on the other hand, was motivated by a desire to recapture
a sense of the authenticity of life that, for Picón Salas, resided in

the environment of the province. Mérida and the land owned by his father had become the homeland of his heart, a "patria entrañable," as he called it (*D*, 1381). The loss of his father's land, which confirmed the need to flee the country, seemed to be the dissolution of all his dreams. It appeared in 1923 that the voyage in search of identity was one that led from one form of disillusionment to another. He felt a sense of abandonment. "It seemed as if the Last Paradise on earth were disappearing in front of my eyes. With the auction and sale, they cut me off from my roots, from that place which I had touched with my hands and trampled with the soles of my feet" (*D*, 1381).

The resiliency of his intellect enabled Picón Salas to compensate for the loss of one ideal by substituting it with another. The concept of a tangible homeland ("patria geográfica") was transformed into a more intellectual and spiritual ideal of integrating himself within the larger cultural homeland ("una patria más grande") of Spanish America (*D*, 1383). Mariano Picón Salas embarked on the ship that would take him to Chile at the Panamanian port city of Cristóbal. Chile, with its history of political moderation and the influence of Andrés Bello in the development of its educational and political institutions, created in Picón Salas the hope of discovering the freedom that he sought.

Essentially, the voyage to Chile was a hope-filled journey. Yet, in the conflict between intellect and emotion—the paradox in the life of Picón Salas—the trip was dominated by a sense of anxiety and nostalgia: an anxiety for the uncertainty experienced by all exiles in the passage from the known to the unknown, and a nostalgia for leaving the homeland of his heart (*patria entrañable*). This nostalgia would never leave the author. Mérida was the nucleus of his existence and would remain as a leitmotiv, an "insistente ritornelo," throughout his prose (*D*, 1382).

On board ship Picón Salas met other intellectuals seeking refuge from the tyranny of dictatorship in their respective countries. He identified with them and proceeded to interpret what he saw to be the fundamental problem of Spanish America: the struggle of modern intellectuals to discover in the culture and history of their countries the source of their own identity. For the intellectual, the problem was choosing between the traditionalism of the past and the values of a technologically more advanced world.

On his way to Chile, Picón Salas envisioned a country that would eventually bring to fruition the political and intellectual

ideals of the young writers and thinkers of the continent. Her
history, beginning with the presidency of Diego Portales in 1831,
demonstrated to the essayist a cultural process which stood in
contradistinction to the despotism and chaos evidenced in the
history of Venezuela and other Latin American countries. Chile,
he thought, had learned to harmonize the disparate elements of
Spanish, English, French, and indigenous cultures represented
in the country; Chile was a unique cultural synthesis. It had absorbed the Enlightenment ideas of Bello and had established the
writ of habeas corpus as the fundamental element in her judicial
system. More so than in any other country, the rights of those who
dissented from the policies of the government were protected by
the laws of the land. For Picón Salas, Chile represented moderation ("harmoniosa mesura") [11] in the formation of her social and
political institutions. Neither conservative nor liberal, Chile
seemed to the author a country in search of synthesis, in search of
the practical application of the theories of Hegel. In the northern
and southern portion of the country there had developed different
cultural phenomena determined by the characteristics of the land
itself; nevertheless, in Chile there appeared to be a balance between order and justice.

In the development of her political system, Chile, contrary to
Venezuela, represented a country that had avoided the institu-
tionalization of the caudillo. Viewing culture as an interaction
between man and his environment, Picón Salas determined
that Chile had been saved from *caudillismo* due to the lack of the
vast expanses of plains regions found in countries like Argentina
and Venezuela. The stereotype of the powerful leader on horseback had had little chance of becoming a reality in the historical
and cultural evolution of the country. The history of Chile, particularly after independence, indicated to Picón Salas that the
pressures of the social group dominated the will of the individual.
Consequently, the leaders of the country were obliged to play the
role of Merovingian kings: the leaders represented in their personality the very people who put them in power.[12] On the other
hand, in Venezuela, the man on horseback, the caudillo, represented no one but himself. Justice under the caudillo was subject to the dictator's personal conception of right and wrong.

In Chile, the institution of *caudillismo* was substituted by the
concept of *el disimulo* ("the art of pretending"), which precluded
the emergence of a leader seeking to divorce himself from the

requisites imposed by the people. The force of group dynamics made it nearly impossible for the rise to power of a Rosas, a Guzmán Blanco, or a García Moreno.[13] In order to rule, the leader had to effect his control over the population in an oblique manner. There had to exist the pretense that the ruler was not really in total control of the country. On the other hand, in the history of Venezuela the caudillo achieved his political preeminence through coercion and by giving the appearance that his human qualities were different and above the rest of the population. More often than not, the caudillo was accompanied, in his visits to the various regions of the country, by an *adivino* (a witch doctor), who added a sense of mysticism to the power of the tyrant.

Picón Salas intuited the element of moderation to be the fundamental characteristic of the Chilean people. This characteristic he saw as an antidote for the tropicalism predominant in the national character of Venezuela. According to the essayist, tropicalism emerged as the influence of the caudillo from the tropical plains areas began to dominate the cultural life of the country after the period of independence.[14] The plainsmen (*llaneros*) brought to the capital mores that opposed the cultural and intellectual environment which prevailed in Caracas in the eighteenth century. Physical strength was valued above intellectual prowess. The bases for the organization of justice under the code of the *llanero* was the concept of the survival of the fittest. In his ignorance, the caudillo attempted to ruralize the urban centers of the country. For the caudillo, ruling a country was not very much different than the art of breaking wild horses. To Picón Salas, the characteristic of tropicalism represented the predominance of passion over reason, lawlessness over justice, and chaos over order. Tropicalism referred to the unbridled spontaneity of passion, and he equated the concept of tropicalism with the expression of individual sexuality—not unlike a spirited stallion (*un potro brioso*) which had to be tamed in order to become productive. In Venezuela the problem was that there had not developed a proper form to mold the irrationalism of the people into a unified concept of national and individual identity.

When the essayist reached Valparaiso in the winter of 1923, the country was in a state of political and social unrest. Five years prior to the author's arrival, the Liberal Alliance (Alianza Liberal), a coalition of radicals, liberal democrats, and Marxists, had achieved its first congressional victory over the power of the

landed aristocracy. About the same time, the economic situation
of the itinerant worker (*rotos*) and rural farm hands (*inquilinos*)
began to worsen. Unemployment became a major factor in the
elections of 1920. With promises to correct the situation, the Alliance managed to get Arturo Alessandri, the Lion of Tarapacá,
elected to the presidency. But the Congress still contained many
conservative elements; it prohibited the president from carrying
out his reforms. The consequence of the stalemate between the
president and Congress was that in 1923 the radical groups with-
drew their support of Alessandri and took their message of revolution to the streets of Valparaiso and Santiago.[15]

Yet there was some indication that a change was taking place in
society. During the first years of the presidency of Alessandri,
office buildings and public housing were constructed. Chile also
seemed on the way to solving her international problems with
neighboring states. As Picón Salas recalled: "There rose up sky-
scrapers, new mining enterprises, socialist parties, and belligerent
associations of workers. . . . Chile prided herself on the cleanliness
of her ships and her abundance of schools. In defiance of false notions of patriotism, the students requested a generous arrange-
ment for Peru, the liquidation of the old Pacific conflict, and a
general policy of Hispanic American brotherhood" (*D*, 1384).

The thirteen years Picón Salas was to spend in Chile represented in the life of the author a maturation of self, his emergence
as a significant literary figure in Spanish America, and the development of a political awareness concerning the relationship
between the individual and the state. Both in Valparaiso, where
he stayed for only a few months, and in Santiago, he discovered
an intellectual atmosphere charged with the rhetoric of new social
theories and revolution. The freedom to express his thoughts was
a new and exciting experience which contrasted sharply with the
oppression he had known in Caracas. He took the opportunity
to describe the Venezuelan tragedy perpetrated by Juan Vicente
Gómez. Chile, at the time, was a kind of Mecca for writers and
intellectuals seeking to transform the political and social situation
of their respective countries: "Never, as in those years, were we
so generous in spirit. We thought that another generation of
independence would come about in order to establish the unity
of our lost continental destiny. Each student who rose to speak
wanted to be, for the moment, the new Bolívar, the new Martí. We

suffered for all of Latin America, which was our blood, be it for the Mexican Revolution or the Nicaraguan Sandino" (*E*, 1392).

While in Valparaiso, Picón Salas gained the friendship of the Chilean novelist Eduardo Barrios. Picón had written an essay on one of Barrios' latest works. The article was published in the literary section of Valparaiso's major newspaper.[16] It evidently appealed to Barrios, for as a return favor he made it possible for the young Venezuelan essayist to be introduced into literary circles of the capital. In Santiago, Picón Salas obtained a position as preceptor at the Pedagogical Institute which permitted him ample time to continue and finish his studies at the National University of Chile. He received a doctoral degree in the Department of Philosophy and Humane Letters. Shortly thereafter he was offered a teaching position at the university. He remained in that position from 1928 to 1936, giving classes in history, aesthetics, and ethics.

He continued to correspond with Alberto Adriani, who at the time had begun his studies in economics, first in Geneva and then in London. In the ensuing correspondence, Picón Salas began to affirm his belief that the essential revolution for changing society rested in the area of education.[17] If as essayist he felt an obligation to explain the nature and meaning of mestizo culture, as teacher he felt actively engaged in the formation of a better future for all of Spanish America. In teaching, Picón Salas discovered the way to combine the aesthetics of literature and the ethics of political action, a political action which, for the essayist, began with the intellectual formation of the individual. In his idealism, Picón Salas developed a Platonic concept of life: the aesthetic value of literature and art could only be determined by the artist's capacity to lead men:

The functions of the artist and the teacher were to develop vocations; to bear witness to awakening souls, to help them on their voyage through the famous regions of the great myths of human destiny. To do all these things is a bit more than just writing, because nothing has as much strength or charismatic appeal as the word or the example. If the writer attires himself with the regalia of culture, the teacher—as I have said for many years—goes daily to the classroom dressed in workmen's cloth to lift up the scaffolding whereby the souls of youth may rise upward toward the attainment of truth and beauty. As much as writing have I loved my teaching profession. (*F*, 1396)

In the essay "Amor, en fin que todo diga y cante" ("Love, So Long as It Tell All), Picón Salas identified the major concern of his generation as an ethical one; it was to discover the proper union between the older values, conventions, and moral repressions and the new perspective of reality that was being developed by the followers of Marx and Freud. For the author, it became obvious that the spirit of romanticism and mysticism which had characterized Latin American creole society was being undermined by the economic realities of Marxian thought and by the fundamental analysis of human intention and deeds offered by Freudian psychology. Picón Salas did not fear the validity of these new realities, but rather the effect that these revelations seemed to be having on the general population. It was one thing to present a new understanding of human existence and behavior; it was quite another to forsake the spiritual and cultural development of the individual in the name of these fundamental realities.

The materialist value system and the theories that reduced men to a common physical denominator, according to Picón Salas, precluded the existence of higher spiritual values and love in human affairs. In the relationship between man and woman, Picón Salas saw the possibility of establishing a communion that transcended mere physical contact. The desire to reach beyond the self and take possession of the world or other self, he said, signified more than just the result of erotic impulses. The force of Eros and the exercise of individual will in directing that force represented the more profound wish to communicate the essence of self to another. Love was a form of sublimation. The reciprocal action of another in complementing the communicative desire of the other produced, he said, the harmony of love. He defined love as "contrapuntal music in which your motif crosses with mine." [18] Love was also a form of pathos, he thought. In the achievement of communion between man and woman each participant in the act of love came to understand the tragic and sublime aspects of human destiny (A, 1407). For Picón Salas, an awareness of the pathos in human life manifests itself through compassion for others.

The existence of love and compassion radiating from the communion between two individuals, in the interpretation of Picón, has a resultant positive effect in the formation of the cultural values of the larger society. This effect he explained in reverse fashion. In those individuals for whom love does not exist there resides the power to destroy the harmony of the world. For those individuals themselves the lack of a harmonious integration between reason and emotion precludes their functioning in the world as men aware of the individuality and integrity of another. Relying only on their personal logic to resolve problems they would impose their will on others and establish a tyranny based on their particular vision of the world. Leaders like Savanarola, Calvin, and Robespierre, said Picón Salas, exemplified men who without compassion sought to remake the world to suit their personal concept of utopia. Without compassion they became demogogues of logic. They became calculating men for whom the easiest way to resolve difficulties was through the use of the guillotine or the firing squad.

According to Picón Salas, the use of logic without compassion finds its justification in reducing the difficulties in life to the least common denominator. However, logic itself cannot establish a sound ethical system. Simply stated, Picón Salas interpreted the tyranny and barbarism in Venezuela as a result of the elimination of compassion and love from the consciousness of the dictator Gómez:

> The cold cruelty of a tyrant like Juan Vicente Gómez can be explained in Venezuela because he never permitted himself to sleep alongside the woman he loved. He took his women like the mule takes fillies without stopping for an instant to understand the nature of fantasy or tenderness. He was always like Holofrenes who feared the unexpected Judith. He substituted the ideal of love in man, which is selective, for the desires of a stud bull. (*A*, 1407)

For Picón Salas, the teacher and essayist, love in the form of compassion enables the individual to identify himself in the social order. It aids in establishing a harmonious relationship between the individual and the rest of society. Unfortunately, politics, by minimizing the introduction of compassion into the consciousness of the people, often mitigates the individual's ability to discover the integrity of self that love brings. For lack of compassion, the particular political ideology sets aside individual rights and considerations in order to change the world according to its utopian vision of perfection. The ideology, then, succeeds in contradicting itself and provides the society with its own series of injustices. It errs in refusing to recognize the spontaneity in life as represented in the individual and his quest for love and identity: "The best Utopia destined to change the world always seems to fall short of its goals when it comes in contact with the reality of human life and the conduct of man. At that point absolute justice breaks up into a series of partial injustices." [19]

For the most part, Picón Salas remained aloof from the practical considerations of politics. Yet for a brief period of time he did help in the organizing of the left-wing Organización Revolucionaria Venezolana along with Rómulo Betancourt. His position in life was that of an intellectual, the principal activity of which he thought to be the search for balance ("una linea de ecuanimidad") between the various ideologies seeking to bring Venezuela and Latin America from chaos to order and justice. Since no political philosophy or previous government in the world had succeeded in establishing a perfect state, he viewed the position of the intellectual as that of an antagonist to the institutions of the state. Nevertheless, he did not request that the intellectual be a political theoretician. Herein lies a paradox of contradiction. While Picón Salas sought to lessen the power of the state, he recognized the need for the state to act affirmatively in order to abolish misery and provide for a more equitable distribution of the riches of the land. He said, however, that it was incumbent upon the intellectual to resist the state when it began to intrude into the area of thought and attempted to direct the spiritual expression of the artist or individual. According to Picón, the individual retained a right recognized by few religious or political dogmas: the right to be heretical. Yet he did not regard this heresy as a negative reply to the institutions of government; it was the result of a Platonic search for harmony between an archetypical world of ideals and reality. He likened the position of the intellectual to that of Don Quixote: "Intellectuals search Platonically for the difficult agreement between the world of archtypes and the world of reality. For example, when Don Quixote freed the galley slaves and then discussed the law which put them in chains, he was breaking the foundation stones on which every imperfect civil unit is built" (V, 1442).

The position assumed by Mariano Picón Salas with respect to the political ideas of both the right and left resembles in form a practical application of the Kantian critique of reason. The author himself admitted to having been influenced by Kant. Picón opposed the dogmatic use of reason and logic in improving the conditions of the world. Ideology, he indicated, only presents a partial image of truth. Opposed to reason was the affective side of man, but in emotion, or passion, man likewise does not comprehend the totality of human existence. The error of the socialists and the Marxists, according to the essayist, was their reliance on logic and reason; the error of the Latin American dictatorships, as manifested through the spirit of the caudillo, was a reliance on passion, or irrationalism, in controlling the destiny of each nation. For Picón Salas a balance, or harmony, between reason and passion had to be established in order to achieve peace between the needs of individuals and those of the larger society.

In an essay on intellectual freedom Picón Salas stated that the state ought not adopt any specific ideology. It should, however, recognize its mission to provide as much freedom for the individual as possible and to offer services as the building of roads, hospitals, schools, and the like.[20] For the most part the essayist saw the perfect state exercising a somewhat passive role in the operation of the society. It was up to the individual in society to control the circumstances of reality. The struggle in life, he continued, was not the social struggle but that of each man to reach beyond material existence and to acquire, as life progresses, love and beauty (metaphysical concepts) which unite him with other men in the search for perfection (a universal ideal).

Disenchanted with the world of politics, Picón Salas looked to culture and education as a way to resolve the dilemma of the Latin American attempting to identify with his environment. He recognized that the reality of historical circumstances often modified the dreams of men. Even Bolívar, he said, in the final stages of life become disillusioned with the disunity and factionalism that followed the struggle for independence. On the other hand, the essayist recognized the impossibility for the intellectual to find total escape from the problems that beset the continent. Picón understood the fundamental need to change the political and economic conditions in Venezuela. It was imperative to free the people from ignorance and poverty if culture and education were to thrive and become meaningful in their lives. His only political platform toward the attainment of these goals was the establishment of an open and democratic society aware of its heritage and the ascending trajectory of history. In the pursuit of social and economic goals, Picón cautioned the intellectuals of America not to sacrifice aesthetic and cultural harmony to politics. He urged the projection of a politics of the Christian spiritual ideals of love and sacrifice into the world of temporal politics. Idealistically, he assumed that in accomplishing such a feat political leaders would be forced to measure their actions by the concept of univeral brotherhood. The author pointed to the European continent, to Switzerland, Denmark, and Holland, in particular, and concluded that their history had not been as violent as that of Venezuela because their tradition of education taught people how to resolve conflict through conciliatory methods. Contrariwise, the tyrant Juan Vicente Gómez capitalized on a weak concept of education in the minds of Venezuelans: for Venezuelans all knowledge rested in their *compadre* Gómez. According to Picón, education, in increasing the cultural and spiritual values of the society, taught men how to maintain a critical posture vis-à-vis the fanaticism of politicians. Only through education and knowledge of culture was it possible to bring about the formation of self.

By 1924 the economic and political situation in Chile had begun to deteriorate for the government of Arturo Alessandri. Nothwithstanding the gains made on behalf of the middle sector of society, the decrease in the international demand for nitrates worsened the economic situation of the lower classes. There developed a stalemate between Alessandri, who had pursued liberal policies during the first years of his presidency, and a more conservative Congress still hoping to reestablish the power of the Fronda aristocrática. The military intervened in this stalemate by staging a successful coup that sent Alessandri into exile. Colonels Carlos Ibañez and Marmaduque Grove took over the reins of government. In March, 1925, the military governors recalled Alessandri from Italy in an attempt to unify right- and left-wing opponents of the government. However, the continuing rise of inflation and unemployment only stimulated further the revolutionary activity of the socialists and the Marxists. Alessandri failed to provide the unity necessary for establishing some sort of national consensus as to what should be done to reverse the downward economic spiral. In October, 1925, Colonel Ibañez headed another coup which returned the country to a military dictatorship that lasted until 1933. In December, 1933, Alessandri reassumed the power of the presidency.[21]

As the economic and political situation in Chile worsened between 1925 and 1933 the essayist became despondent regarding the possibilities of establishing in Latin America a just and free society. In Venezuela the power of the dictator Gómez appeared more solidified and more lasting than ever. Notwithstanding a student rebellion and earthquake in Cumaná in 1928, the dictator enhanced his position in the world with emphasis on the production of oil and the building of roads. In 1930, when the rest of the world was suffering the effects of the Great Depression, Gómez made it possible for Venezuela to be the only country in the hemisphere to pay its public debt through the oil proceeds. The paying of the debt in that year was doubly significant, for 1930 was also the centenary anniversary of the independence of the country. For the festivities, dignitaries from around the world were invited; the international press applauded the country (and Gómez) for its accomplishment during a period of economic decline in the rest of the world.

Picón wondered whether or not it would be necessary to await the death of the caudillo in order for a change to take place in Venezuela. He also reflected on what he considered to be the decline in the quality of life in Chile. He saw that decline multiplied in Venezuela. What had happened to the aspirations of the student movements of 1913 and 1919? What had happened to his own generation, many of whom had gone back to Venezuela to live, as he put it, floating on the dead waters of days without hope or illusions? He saw in the modern world the proliferation of a materialistic ethic corrupting whole generations of men. In Venezuela, he said, there existed only two types of men: those who were ignorant of the extent of the power and capacities of the dictator and those who, while aware of the evils of Gómez, supported his power for the material benefits afforded by the alliance that Venezuela had with United States oil companies: "Men are divided into those who are stupid and those who live. Stupid are those who think that Gómez is mortal and that in this beaten land of ours a more just and healthier regime will be created. Alive are those who after visiting Maracay change the licence plates of their automobiles." [22] He wondered about the conscience of the rest of the world that refused to acknowledge the lack of civilized government in his country. To Picón Salas, it seemed that no one cared about the fate of Venezuelans: "From the massive walls of Gómez' jails, in the silence of the dark night, one can hear the cries of tortured men. One, two, three, the guard makes his round and the sound of the whip cracks against the cold shoulders of fear. Who hears them? For the civilized world the Gómez regime is also a civilized regime. The newspapers everyday sing the same song: Peace, wealth, and the Meritorious One" (R, 361).

The thought of possibly never being able to return to Venezuela and the effects of the military dictatorship of Colonel Ibañez in Chile precipitated, in Picón Salas, for the first time, the idea of leaving the country. In 1930 he sent a letter to Don Joaquín García Monge in Costa Rica; in 1932 to Nieto Caballero in Colombia. He inquired about the political climate in their respective countries and whether or not it would be advisable to reestablish himself in either place. The negative replies he received cast him further into a state of depression. Life became fastidious. In his position as librarian in the National Library—teaching was a part-time job—he felt that he was vegetating. He saw in Chile, with the third administration of Alessandri, an alliance between the president and the military that could only lead to one of two things: a revolution fermented by socialist dogmatists or a military fascism. In a letter he wrote: "The time is dark. A time of suspicion, of hatred, of spiritual depression. A time very characteristic of a revolution now aborted." [23]

During the late 1920s and early thirties, Picón Salas began to formulate his ideas on revolution. It became obvious, at that time, that in order for Latin America to become part of the modern world, radical change in the structure of society had to be effectuated. The question was how was such a change to come about. For many of the intellectuals the answer was to be found in the Marxian concept of revolution. For some, the advance of technology itself would alleviate the burdens of the lower classes in the society. For others, like Mariano Picón Salas, the revolution had to be a revolution in education.

Picón Salas categorically opposed those who advocated the theories of the socialists and Marxists. His criticism was that these revolutionaries possessed a static concept of history. He saw that the world was changing and that the power of the industrial magnates was slowly diminishing. The problem with the adherents of Marx, those whom he met while living in Chile, was that they viewed the development of Western history through the eyes of Marx. Rather than being revolutionaries in favor of change, Picón Salas viewed these theorists as anachronistic in their approach to economic and social problems. Furthermore, the basic interpretation of the course of history, according to the

Marxists, stood in opposition to that of Picón. While the Marxist envisioned the ultimate synthesis of historical change in the dictatorship of the proletariat, the essayist understood the Hegelian concept of change to be a continual and never-ending process. Besides, for Picón Salas, a dictatorship of any kind represented an anathema to the development of the individual.

Unlike the Marxists, the writer emphasized the role of the individual in society. He saw in the myth of Prometheus the eternal symbol of man. Prometheus had defied the gods, and this defiance symbolized the existence of the will of man that strikes out against any form of tyranny. The myth of Prometheus demonstrated the loneliness of existence and the anguish and doubts that are constantly present in human life. Where the Marxist attempted to restrain the expression of free will, Picón saw in Prometheus' challenge the need for the individual to challenge the immediacy of his circumstance as soon as that circumstance should begin to inhibit his freedom to express himself.

For the essayist, the goal of man is absolute freedom, as it is, also, the goal of society. But the society can only be free if the individuals within it are free to direct its course. The fundamental reality that has to be taken into consideration when determining the structure of society is that the individual, given his freedom, constantly sets out on new voyages in search of the unknown: "The possibility of man dominating the world is never better illustrated than when we analyze with a free will the conflicts in life and the human circumstance; than when we can undertake a voyage like that of Ulysses to that place where the sea seems untouched by human hand and the vision of the navigator is prepared for every surprise." [24]

To Picón, the socioeconomic theories that prevailed in Latin America sought to limit the peregrination of the individual. True, life was a material struggle to achieve greater comforts, but in the myth of Prometheus the essayist interpreted the need to discover the spiritual identity of the individual. The peregrination, or *errancia,* into the unknown represented to Picón Salas the search for ideals. Revolution for him was a revolution of the spirit of man in order to determine his own destiny: "The idea of Revolution was for me to arrive much further than to that hermetic Paradise which was called the dictatorship of the proletariat." [25]

The author attacked the Marxists, calling them the demons

("endemoniados") of history. He picked up the phrase from his
reading of Dostoevski and used it to indicate their irrationalism
in the formulation of their extreme theories. In the Marxian
concept of revolution, Picón saw the advocacy of the liquidation
of the past. This idea contrasted sharply with his vision of the
need to resurrect the cultural past in order to ascend toward the
acquisition of utopia.

In Latin America, for example, Picón traced the present desire
for freedom as part of the historical legacy that began even before
the days of independence. He saw the present as part of the historical continuum of time. If revolution were to be meaningful in
Latin America, he thought that it would be necessary to comprehend the past and to extract from history those elements useful
in projecting a positive vision of the future. He saw that the values
of people are part of the historical legacy and in assessing those
values he traced their trajectory beginning with the earliest
civilizations. The past could not be jettisoned, because it is
through the past that the present acquires meaning. Without the
past, he thought, life would proceed like the cycles of nature,
containing a beginning and an end with no apparent goal in
mind. Marxism was simplistic and lacking knowledge of the
intricacies of life and history: "It was as if someone had substituted
for me an unadorned wall made of lime for a brilliant tapestry"
(L, 1413).

In Santiago de Chile, Picón Salas frequented literary gatherings
in the homes of Eduardo Barrios, Armando Donoso, and Sara
Hubner. The poet that most impressed him was Pablo Neruda.
In Neruda, Picón discovered a sense of the vague and lamenting
sensuality that sleeps in the soul of the mestizo ("la vaga y herida
sensualidad que duerme en el alma mestizo") (F, 1389). The
significance of this discovery was important to him for as an
essayist he had established for himself the goal of uncovering the
myths and truths that structured the mentality of the Latin
American creole. In Registro de huéspedes (Guest Registry),
published in 1934, he stated his objectives as follows: "To hit
upon that undecided serpentine and secret truth which is like
one of these nocturnal rural contrysides where the discredited
moon still offers its teeth made of garlic to dogs." In the poetry
and in the voice of Neruda, he saw represented the subsurface
reality of the history of the continent. He saw the agony and the
pathos that produced the mestizo race and wondered how he

was going to comprehend it completely: "How was I going to identify the voice and poetry of that man whose land weeps and overflows in the south of Chile, and from which one can hear the sound of the 'trutruca,' that large trumpet which the Araucanian Indian blows with a cosmiclike sound in the forests" (*F*, 1392).

For Picón Salas the poetry of the early period of Neruda represented an expression of the common humanity in all men, a universal concept which Picón in his own essays attempted to describe. Neruda seemed to understand the tragedy of Latin America in the disunity between man and his environment. Picón also identified with the errant spirit of the poet that took him to far off places like Madrid, India, and Java in order to better understand the fundamental characteristics of all men.

In Neruda's poetry Picón Salas also discovered a concept of the limitlessness of human experience. Each particular activity of man represents the potential of man. For Picón Salas the concept of *errancia* incorporated the challenge of the individual to the limitations of immediate circumstance.

Between 1929 and 1932 the essayist became involved in founding two literary magazines. The first, in 1929, was called *Letras*, and was edited in collaboration with Salvador Reyes and Hernán del Solar. With the second, *Indice*, the more important of the two, Picón had the collaboration of Eugenio González, Ricardo Latcham, Raul Silva Castro, and Juan Gómez Millas. Unfortunately, little information is available about this magazine or the effect it had in orienting the intellectual community toward a specific viewpoint about art and culture. Siso Martínez mentions in his book *Mariano Picón Salas* that the Chilean writer Hector Fuenzalida has documented this work of Picón Salas in Chile in a collection of letters.[26] To date, however, I have not been able to locate these letters. For Picón Salas, at least, the intention of those associated with *Indice* was important enough for him to include the preamble, written by him, in the first edition of his book, *Intuición de Chile* (*Intuition of Chile*).

The purpose of *Indice*, as stated by Picón Salas, paralleled the personal sense of mission and duty he felt as a writer and teacher to serve the society and country of which he was a part. The difference between his essays and the magazine was merely that the efforts in *Indice* represented a collectivist undertaking by a group of intellectuals attempting to reevaluate the cultural situation of man in Latin America. The difference between *Indice* and other

literary periodicals was that the former left the door open for all
aesthetic and sectarian views which contained any truth, judg-
ment, or concept of beauty aspiring to the attainment of timeless
Platonic ideals. The main contentions of the group responsible
for *Indice* was that life in Latin America had come to lack pro-
fundity, certitude, and faith in the work of the individual, and
that in an attempt to do all things at once in order to catch up
to the pace of the technologically advanced countries, Latin
Americans had lost contact with the fundamental reality and
cultural values of the continent. Artificiality and pretentiousness
had been substituted for authenticity. The material things in life
had come to determine man instead of man determining the nature of things. The mission of *Indice* was to reintegrate man and
his environment through a comprehension of culture as "una
cultura vital." In order to realize this goal it was necessary, at
first, to provide a basic understanding of the underlying forces
that resided in the internal structure of Latin American culture.
In this way the concept of culture would not be limited to the
elitist concept of culture as a European import and ornament for
personal use only. The interpretation of culture in *Indice*
descended from Platonic heights to define the immediacy of the
Latin American environment in order that man in this environment might return in an ascent toward more eternal values.

The significance of *Indice* in the peregrination of Picón Salas
is that it provided the basis for the cultural activity that he was
to realize in Venezuela after 1936. In founding the *Revista
Nacional de Cultura* in 1938, Picón Salas, in the prologue to the
first edition, restated the goals first expressed in *Indice*.

IV   *Return to Venezuela*

The dictator Juan Vicente Gómez died on December 17, 1935,
and the new government that came to power was headed by
Gómez' minister of war and navy, General Eleazar López Contreras. In April, 1936, López Contreras became the first president
in Venezuela's history. He was to hold office for a five-year period
after which national elections would be held to elect by popular
ballot the first elected president of the country. The initial policies
of the new government in 1936 gave the appearance that Venezuela was on a path that would lead to the establishment of a
democratic tradition. López Contreras even went as far as creating

a national ideology based on the principles and ideals of Simón Bolívar. The intellectuals, many living in exile, began to filter back into Venezuela and some, like Alberto Adriani and Rómulo Gallegos, were given important positions in the governmental hierarchy: Adriani became the minister of agriculture and was later named treasurer of the nation; Rómulo Gallegos became minister of education. After three months Gallegos was replaced by Arturo Uslar Pietri.[27]

The problem of the returning émigrés, as indicated by Mariano Picón Salas, was one of reintegrating themselves into the mainstream of national life. In Venezuelan history, the precursor of independence, Francisco de Miranda, served as a prime example of the emotional and psychological problems facing the exiled patriot upon returning to the country. Miranda, who had set out from Venezuela in search of light, liberty, and utopia for his country, discovered upon his return an attitude of reserve and ill will ("reticencia y encono") from those who had remained living in Caracas and in Coro (*Re*, 1424). As a prototype, Miranda, in the trajectory of his peregrination throughout the world, symbolized for Picón Salas the confrontation between the cosmopolitanizing effect of *errancia* and the isolationism of those Venezuelans who continued to believe in the traditions and legends of the country.[28] He stated: "With ideas like harpoons, and arrowlike dreams on the high seas one fights against the prejudice and ignorance which darkens our country" (*Re*, 1424).

In 1936 the change in the political situation of the country did not make the process of reintegration any easier for the exiled intellectual. To an extent, that change made the problem of the émigré all the more difficult to handle. The new political situation elevated hopes that the time had come when dreams of utopia for the nation would finally come to fruition. Upon reentering the country, however, the intellectual discovered an attitude of rejection on the part of the rest of society.

In *Mundo imaginario,* published two years before his return to Venezuela, Picón Salas personalized the problem of reintegration through the figure of a relative who, years before, had left Mérida in search of fortune in the rubber plantations of Brazil. The acquisition of a different behavioral pattern, a different mode of dress, and the introduction in his speech of uncustomary sounds contrasted vigorously with the routine and traditional way of life that, for the most part, had not changed during his absence. The relative had become a stranger in his own land: "He is a stranger in the house where everyone has appeared to have partaken in the same labors. Life, which interrupted itself for a moment with his arrival, now continues its natural course. My uncles go to their business, my aunts to their devotions, and the grandfather copies his stories in his *Big Book*. Every year that passes with its twelve long months—1894, 1895, 1896—are in the grandfather's book. Only for the recently arrived guest time seems divided and touches an emptiness." [29]

The horror and silence that Gómez had imposed upon the country between 1908 and 1935 had become a natural phenomenon in the minds of the people. It compared to the routine in the change of seasons. The atmosphere of ignorance and fear that sustained the power of the dictator had produced in Venezuela two classes of intellectuals: the sad and defeated idealists, who eventually succumbed to the theory of a national and organic fatalism in explaining Gómez' rule, and the imprisoned, who had dared to question Gómez' right to rule. The rest of the society merely obeyed the dictates of Gómez and immersed themselves in the routines and problems of daily living. The spiritual fatalism that Picón Salas identified as a legacy of the colonial past had degenerated into the notion that suffering, both spiritual and physical suffering, was an expression of manhood: "To suffer or to make suffer, sadistically, was proof of manhood" (*Re*, 1426). In the minds of the people, it appeared that the historical past and present were joined in a painful struggle comparable to that between rider and beast in a rodeo: "Even the friendship and the alliance of the *cuadillos* seemed too much like the way in which riders in a rodeo emulate one another. Let's see who can be the first to overthrow the beast. To mount the saddle in a certain way, to control the prancing horse and dominate the arena were signs of a daring sense of individuality. Comrade Monagas deposed comrade Páez, and in spite of the latter's grey hairs and his heroism, the former threw him in jail. Comrade Gómez deposed comrade Castro" (*Re*, 1426). For those who had lived through the terror and arbitrary incarcerations there was a feeling of resentment toward the intellectuals who had escaped Gómez' reign of terror.

Picón Salas saw the antagonism that developed between the returning émigrés and those who stayed to suffer the tragedy as a perceptual one with regard to the country. Having escaped the tyranny of the dictator and no longer direct witnesses to the problems of hunger, frustration, fatigue, anguish, and superstition, the intellectuals living in exile had developed an abstract notion of the country. Contrary to the utopian dreams of the intellectuals, the reality of life within the country resided in the concrete problems represented by individuals named Pedro, Felipe, Carlos. In order to survive, they had had to accommodate themselves to the will of the dictator; they now had to go on believing in the stereotype of the caudillo. The question that arose in the mind of Picón Salas on his way back to Caracas was which of the two perceptions of the country best described the authenticity of life. While the people were forced to control their existence through the irrationalism of their passions and needs, the intellectual was developing a more rational vision of *patria* which, perhaps, only existed as a fiction.

The road which led from the port city of La Guaria to Caracas in 1936 differed markedly from the Quixotic voyage of the essayist to Caracas in 1920. The first trip was initiated by a sense of adventure and the desire to discover new realities; the second was a journey of reflection. To Picón Salas, it paralleled the situation of the retired mariner, who, once he has left the ship, is forced to remember for better or worse, the trajectory of his expedition through life.[30] Even before returning to Venezuela, Picón Salas stated in *Registro de huéspedes* that "Life is not like an ideal nocturnal countryside dreamed during adolescence, but a municipal road, made of stone, without poetry, and many kilometers long which wears out our hearts and the soles of our shoes." [31] Life, he said, was a struggle against indifference in which each one vainly attempts to communicate his personal vision of reality to another: "To live is like seeing faces pass by in a pulsating metropolis near Forty-second street in New York and between lighted street signs and commercial advertisements" (*M*, 1446). At twenty years of age the idealism of youth perceives a better world run by men of culture. In time youth becomes aware that the world is not governed by idealism, but by the cunning and shrewdness of those in power.

The trip from La Guaira to Caracas, in a sense, was a descending journey from the vision of the country as a potential utopia to the harsh and narrow limitations of concrete reality. It was a trip of reflection and nostalgia. In considering the history of the country, Picón was torn between thoughts of what could have been

and what the reality of that history was. He saw reflected in the
countryside between La Guaira and Caracas the disillusionment
and suffering that had characterized events for more than a century: "A countryside of greatness torn asunder; of red hill tops
which have bled and suffered throughout the history of the nation;
of clouds in rebellion, strewn against the sky; of chasms which
shield the cactus like disheveled indigenous soldiers" (*Re*, 1427).

The desire to reintegrate himself and participate, once again,
in the life of the country took precedence over any other consideration. There existed in the consciousness of the essayist the
idea that he had, to an extent, lost contact with the fundamental
reality of his own identity. He wished to rediscover the lyricism
of youth when the world seemed to await the challenge of a
Quixotic spirit; he needed to reestablish contact with his native
soil and renew old relationships: "Just for a moment it is necessary to smell the earth; absorb the arrowlike glances of its tropical sun; drag lost images through one's memory; see traces of
ourselves in the countenances of our relatives and friends who
come to receive us and who are twelve years older; and crawl, like
in a river, through the adventure of our own experience"
(*Re*, 1427). For Picón Salas, the process of reintegration with
Venezuelan reality was fundamentally a reintegration with the
identity of self.

For a brief period of time the López Contreras government
opened up the political process to all ideologies in the political
spectrum. However, there developed a contrast between those
who sought fundamental social and economic reforms and those
who only wished to enhance their political prestige with the new
government. Picón Salas saw the atmosphere of Caracas as
charged with a renewed aggression of political rhetoric that reduced men to labels: bourgeois, reactionary, or Communist. He
preferred to see men judged in the fullness of their humanity. The
political labeling, on the other hand, seemed to him to perpetuate
the dehumanization of society: "We call them reactionaries or
revolutionaries as if they were of a zoological order. We could
call them vertebrae, invertebrae, cuadripedes, or anthropoids"
(*Re*, 1431). He viewed each political group as modern-day
pharisees discerning the reality of life in terms of their own
particular dogmas. Each political group became locked in its
particular vision of life and reduced metaphysical concepts to the
liturgy and routine of political speech-making.

Although the period of institutionalized violence and barbarism had ended, there now existed a more subtle and indirect type of intellectual barbarism that prohibited the flourishing of universal, ethical, and aesthetic cultural values. Without harmony and balance between passion and intellect culture could not survive. The Venezuela of 1936 still awaited the period of national reconciliation: "Culture must wait the time of the reconciliation of brothers. It is necessary to lay down the road of literacy for the multitudes who are still unable to read. A system of values will then be forged to combat the violence and despotism" (*Re*, 1432).

CHAPTER 6

Europe and America

I Picón's Overview

WITHIN a year after his return to Caracas Picón Salas was assigned the diplomatic post of chargé d' affairs in Prague. The literary result of his residency in Europe was a series of essays entitled *Preguntas a Europa: Viajes y ensayos* (*Questions Put to Europe: Trips and Essays*), published in 1937. Ten years later, after Picón had spent some time in the United States, he published a revised and expanded version entitled *Europa-América: Preguntas a la esfinge de la cultura*, (*Europe-America: Questions Put to the Sphinx of Culture*). The essays contained in this book represent an ever-increasing expansion of the author's views on world affairs and his unique talent for critical observation. He demonstrates an ability to synthesize, through the use of metaphor and vignette, the cultural essences of those countries he visited. Consistent with his ideas on the essay as a literary genre, *Europa-América* is a reaction to the apparent social and cultural disintegration of Europe which presaged the coming of World War II.

More in the vein of a poet-historian than a political commentator on world events, Picón Salas, in this book, seeks to come to grips with universal humanistic values and mankind's eternal struggle between the creative forces of his intellect and the destructive forces of human instinct. The first part of *Europa-América* is an intellectual journey in search of those positive elements in societal development which might expand culture and civilization. Or to state it as Picón Salas did, the book confronts what he called the sphinx of culture for answers to the riddle of civilization which, while promoting the creative powers of man, at times sets in motion those mechanistic forces which lead to its own destruction.

100

The essays contained in the second part of the book show that the author is deeply concerned with the future of political and cultural relations between the United States and Latin America. We encounter, once again, the author's search for those cultural values which might create harmony among nations and different societies. In dealing with the American continent, Picón Salas examines both the negative and positive aspects of each culture and emphasizes those cultural values which fit within the larger cultural framework of the Western tradition. In so doing, Latin America, the United States, and Europe are seen as products of a long historical and cultural process rather than as separate political entities.

What we might define as an essential unity in the essays is the author's personal identification with the anguish and suffering experienced by a world caught up in the throes of war and being driven to the point of self annihilation. The world, as Picón saw it in the 1930s and 1940s, was a world confronted by the destructive forces of the Antichrist. While the mythological figure of the Antichrist specifically symbolized Nazi tyranny, Picón saw the rise to power of the Antichrist as the result of a world that had substituted its ethical and spiritual values for a dehumanized materialism and technology. Nonetheless, Picón Salas interpreted the European crisis as an opportunity for the Western world to reach a new cultural synthesis, a synthesis based on Christian moral principles and a better notion of the need for all men to establish a sense of international brotherhood.

Europa-América is also a response to an identity crisis, which Picon considered as responsible for the cultural disintegration of Europe and for the inability of Latin Americans to resolve their internal political problems. If, on the one hand, the Europeans had sought to disregard the traditional ethical values of their past for the material pragmatism of industrialization, on the other, the Latin Americans had failed to understand much about the roots of their own cultural heritage. For the Venezuelan author his trip to Europe represented, as he stated, a trip to discover the roots of his Latin American identity in the countryside and cultures of different peoples. Seen from this perspective, *Europa-América* is both a subjective and objective search for the answer to the riddle of civilization.

To begin with, the essayist identifies culture as part of an evolutionary process springing from the development of urban society. In the 1970s such a definition of culture might fall into disrepute with sociologists and anthropologists. But it must be remembered that Picón Salas does not approach the subject from a scientific point of view. His interpretation of culture is more like that of the philosopher or poet, who instead may be in search of the ethical and aesthetic notion of culture. As the development of urban society could be plotted on an evolutionary chart, so too, according to Picón, might the process of cultural development be considered an evolutionary one. Yet it did not follow in Picón's views of society and mankind that this evolutionary process was determined by some natural law; the process was rather the direct expression of man's will to improve the human condition. Where social and economic inequities did exist in society, Picón Salas was more prone to interpret these injustices as the result of the breakdown of moral values.

Picón explained the overall quality of life in Europe in 1939 as a form of cultural Darwinism in reverse. In his view, the pursuit of knowledge and culture had become subordinate to the struggle for power by those who advocated political ideologies through the application of brute force. Contrary to human experience, said Picón, the political myths of Fascism, Nazism, Marxism, and Falangism—all of which were important and growing during the 1930s in Europe—had succeeded in voiding the lesson of history which had taught men for centuries that truth was an ideal to be constantly pursued. Consequently, said the author, the freedom and dignity of the individual was being subjugated to the rhetoric of party discipline. What all this meant to Picón was that the European cultural and political process, which had liberated men from tyranny in the past, had now reversed itself. Europe in the twentieth century had begun to resurrect the same destructive forces in society which once had destroyed the ancient city of Babylon.

Picón said that in order for man in the Western world to overcome the negative political and economic influences of the twentieth century he would have to reconstruct a view of culture and civilization as more than the result of material progress and technological advancement. The writer maintained that technology was not an end unto itself, but an instrument to be used by man to improve the human condition. He also feared that the imposition of a materialistic approach to life through pragmatism was aiding in the development of a notion of culture as a natural or mechanistic phenomenon and not an act of human will. If mankind were to conform to the current cultural mold established by party rule, man would no longer seek to answer important questions of conscience in directing his life.

In order to counter the negative aspects of the technological age, Picón advocated that mankind continue to cultivate a notion of spiritual revolution. As interpreted by the essayist, cultural evolution was the result of a constant confrontation between man and his environment. Once man realizes that the struggle is real, he sees that he is obligated to choose between varying value structures. He then realizes that it is his responsibility to direct the formation of his society toward the establishment of a spiritually meaningful life and a more perfect cultural entity. Man also has the responsibility to learn from other men and to work with others toward the formation of a better world. Furthermore, according to the author, this state of perfection could only be achieved in a democratic society in which all men were free to develop their talents and ideas without interference from the state.

Picón Salas identified the European failure to continue toward the development of a society in which political harmony and justice would reside as the result of the rise of nationalism. To him, nationalism was an anathema to these goals because it precluded the acquisition of a cosmopolitan view of life and knowledge about the universality in man's spiritual nature. Picón interpreted man's spiritual nature as knowledge concerning the spiritual geography of life. Europe, he said, had once possessed, during the Roman Empire and later during the Renaissance, such a spiritual geography. However, he continued, she had lost that awareness of life in succumbing to nationalism; Europe had lost her spirituality. As a result she had lost her ability to perceive life spontaneously; the growth process stopped and in her stagnant state Europe lost her sense of hope in the future. She then resorted to the barbaric means of war as a way to resolve her unhappiness.

Latin America, on the other hand, had not yet developed a spiritual sense of life. Since the Conquest, the cultural process of life had not proceeded in any logical fashion. If the Europeans had succumbed to the rhetoric of political ideologies in creating the barbarism of war, in Latin America a cultural wasteland had been created due to the emphasis on the use of human instinct in

creating the various nation states. The essayist implied that there
did not exist in the Latin American countries a contemporary
awareness of an ethical tradition which could act as a harmonizing
force in resolving internal conflict, and thus Latin America
faced its own kind of stagnation.

II *France*

Of all the European nations analyzed in *Europa-América*,
France is seen as the model of cultural harmony and synthesis.
Picón did not mean to say that France had not experienced
chaotic periods in her history. He concluded, however, that the
French people had learned how to convert their revolutionary
spirit into a principle of moderation as the nation developed.
The French nation, he said, represented a harmonious fusion
between passion and reason. Unlike the Latin Americans, the
French had profited by their mistakes. Picón was attracted to
French success in uniting the aesthetic responses to life of
romanticism and classicism. In his opinion, French culture
represented the fusion between the indecision and spontaneity of
the Germanic people and the clarity of thought and vision of the
peoples of southern Europe. As an example, Picón identified the
figure of Madame Bovary walking aimlessly and depressed
through the streets of Paris under the shadow of the classical
structures of French cathedrals.[1] He saw the juxtaposition of these
two contrasting elements as representing a sense of spiritual
union and moderation. In spite of her internecine wars, France
was able to work out her problems within a structure which in
time represented the development of a new cultural synthesis.

In Picón's view of life, moderation as a cultural value was
necessary in order for a people to harmonize their institutions
with their environment. In France, moderation manifested itself
in the way in which her people worked toward the attainment of
national goals. France, according to Picón, after the destruction of
the monarchy in the eighteenth century, did not permit herself to
be ruled by factionalism. Latin America, on the other hand, did
not unite after independence, but split into eighteen different
countries most of which were further factionalized by the ambi-
tions of local dictators. Whereas Picón characterized the French
historical experience as one of continuity in time, he saw the

Latin American experience as one of *acaso,* a series of chance happenings.

For Picón Salas the French characteristic of moderation possessed a moral value structure in which the impulses of instinct become subject to an eternal law of rhythm. He further stated that for any nation to identify itself and to progress it had to discover its own particular rhythm or balance between reason and instinct. The discovery of such a rhythm, he said, enables a people to creatively fuse the results of calculating intelligence with the desires of blind passion. As a result, France had succeeded in developing a tolerant attitude toward individual ideas along with a universal sense of freedom and justice. While other people had become accustomed to viewing history as external to individual action, French historians have consistently sought to illustrate history through the plight of the individual.

In order for Latin Americans to incorporate into their emotional and psychological development the universal principles of moderation, Picón hoped that Latin American thinkers would establish spiritual enclaves where people would examine their own conscience and the conscience of the nation. The only solution for change in Latin America was to provide a means by which men's souls would be transformed.

In this essay on France, we can easily discern that Picón Salas was in search of a new spiritual awareness of life which would enable man to blend the internal needs of his soul with the material needs of his body. Concerning the relationship between man and society, the essayist sought to harmonize the relationship between the vitality of life—society—and the goals of the individual.

III Germany

In the essay entitled *Meditación alemana (Thoughts on Germany)*, Picón Salas identified Germany of the 1930s as representing the antithesis of cultural harmony. He condemned Germany's pursuit of military goals and the political organization of the country during the thirties which was resurrecting the myth of the Antichrist. But the problem, said Picón, was not merely the result of contemporary materialism. Germany, he continued, similar to the Aztec civilization, had long ago es-

tablished its cultural tradition on blood myths. German civilization was grounded on the concept of the limitless use of personal
will. Her early myths glorified a dependence on man's instincts
in shaping the world. What did occur in German mythology,
according to Picón, and that which did not occur in Greek or
Roman antiquity, was that the Germanic people had forgotten to
give anthropomorphic form to the gods. Consequently, Picón
Salas surmised, the individual in German society understood the
power of his own will as corresponding to the will of the gods.
Hitler was the most notorious representation of this phenomenon.
It was true, he said, that the southern European countries had
occasionally developed grandiose notions of empire. However,
southern cultures did not perceive the concept of idealism for
the sake of the ideal, something that the German philosopher
Keyserling said existed in the German pysche; German idealism
interpreted the divine principles of life as inherent in the blood of
the German people.[2]

According to Picón Salas, Germany had developed a culture
which emphasized the instinctual needs of man. The result, was a
political organization in the twentieth century designed to satisfy
those passions along the limited lines of personal pride. He
compared the quest for personal power in German politics with
that of Latin America's dictators and cited Juan Perón as a prime
example of a man driven to excessive use of power acquired
through instinct. All nations, he said, had the responsibility to
choose between a value structure based on personal need and
passion, or one of moderation which would provide for the needs
of all men. For Picón Salas, the Venezuelan in search of a cultural
identity, Germany was a living symbol of an historical experience
which Latin Americans had to avoid as they strove to create their
own future.

IV *Italy*

Italian art and architecture represented to Picón Salas the
quintessential balance between the classical preocupation with
the practical aspects of structural form and the romantic need to
express within a given structure the feeling and emotions of the
individual artist. As the essayist reviewed the cultural process of
Italian civilization he observed that it is possible to perceive the

existence of a great energy in the palaces and art of the Renaissance.[3] Had it not been for the emphasis, at the same time, on form
and structure, this creative energy would have unleashed itself in
a destructive rather than a productive way. The history of Italian
art, said Picón, represents the internal struggle between the reason and the passion of Italian painters of the fifteenth century.
He noted that there existed a greater expression of romantic impulses than even during the period of romanticism in other
European countries. Picón stated that during the romantic period
much of the apparent expression of passion was contrived. Such
was not the case in Italian Renaissance art. Concealed within the
preoccupation with form, it is possible, according to the essayist,
to sense the great passions and energy which characterize the
Italian quest for life.

Unlike Germanic culture, Italian culture did not permit the
expression of egocentric drives to dominate the society. Whereas
the German cultural experience reacted to an interpretation
based on forebodings of an eventual holocaust which would
annihilate human existence, the Italians had established a
reverence for life. For the Italian, said Picón, life was a more
joyous adventure. Death too had a different psychological effect on the Italians than it did on the Germans: in German culture, according to Picón, death was a cruel conclusion to the
vitality of life which had to be expressed at all costs, whereas
in the Italian view death demonstrated the need to enjoy life with
others.

V *Spain*

According to Picón Salas, the significance of Spanish culture
for the Latin American in search of his identity is that Spain
offers a fundamental understanding concerning the interaction
between man and his environment. Even during the industrial
period, Spain had consistently been concerned more with the
spiritual development of the individual than with improving his
economic position in life. To illustrate this point, Picón said that
while the beggar in England is ashamed of his lot, for it represents
a kind of social regression, in Spain the beggar perceives himself
as an unemployed nobleman. In Spanish society, no man has to
feel humiliated because of his particular socioeconomic condi-

tion. Each man has a place in the world. The Spanish view of life, said Picón, is based on the notion that all men are equal before God.

In dealing with the Spanish Civil War of the 1930s Picón said that while other European nations were concerned about how to control their neighbors through the use of force, Spain was involved with the task of discovering her identity in a world in which many of her traditions no longer seemed valid. Spain was attempting to exorcise from herself those superstitions and fears which had prevented her from participating in the social and economic progress evident in other countries. Spain was in search of a new history for herself. The Spanish social crisis of the 1930s represented, said Picon, a kind of cultural catharsis. The difficult question facing Spain was how to become part of the contemporary scene and at the same time hold on to her idealism as manifested in Spain's notion of chivalry.

Unlike Spain, many of the other European countries had long abandoned the chivalric ideal. The chivalric peregrination in search of truth was substituted for the quest for material goods and money. For Picón Salas, the chivalric spirit represented the aspiration toward the attainment of humanistic ideals; the materialistic quest, a quest derived from impulse. According to the author's perspective of life, the net result of the substitution of material values over spiritual ones is that in contemporary society man is no longer judged for what he is but for what he possesses.[4] Contemporary man has become a collector of goods which define him. Picón Salas believed this development in man's outlook to be a tragedy, a tragedy in which the individual detaches himself from the very essence of his existence and begins to associate the significance of life with the objects society produces.

The value of Spanish culture for Latin America was that Spain was still trying to sustain the relevance of a Quixotic view of life. Don Quixote was still alive in Spain in the 1930s. Picón Salas also believed that material progress was not diametrically opposed to the spiritual nobility represented by the errant knight. He thought that both the material and spiritual views of life could coexist in the world. Like the individual, each nation had the responsibility of discovering the spirit in the body, and by so doing, struggle. This was what was happening or had happened in Spain.

VI *Czechoslovakia*

Czechoslovakia made a lasting impression on Picón Salas. He interpreted the historical struggle of her people for self-determination as a search for religious and political independence. It was from the ranks of the underprivileged classes during the Middle Ages that there developed in the Czech people the notion of political autonomy and the desire to pursue certain religious ideals in order to prevent their subjugation by foreign rulers. Such leaders as Jan Amos Comenius, Jan Hus, and Thomas Masaryk, who arose from the most humble beginnings, were able to rally the people in common cause against the injustice and totalitarianism imposed by invaders like the Hapsburgs and Hitler.[5]

Picón saw in the struggle of the Czech people a moral lesson for Latin Americans. As had occurred in Czechoslovakia, an intelligencia had to rise from the working class in Latin America. Before this could happen, however, the underprivileged in Latin America had to develop a spiritual sense of their own worth. Picón observed that it was in the rural regions of Bohemia where the Czech soul was formed. Generation after generation the peasants of this region were forced to suffer the indignities imposed upon them by the ruling class. What was significant to Picón Salas was that these people never lost a sense of their own integrity. They maintained pride in their traditions and in themselves and waited for the precise moment to revolt. As a result, the Czech national character, which developed out of subjugation, never directed its energies toward the subjugation of others. The Czech people, according to Picón, succeeded in harmonizing their religious ideals with their political goals in the pursuit of democratic principles.

VII *The United States*

Picón Salas left Europe with a sense of disappointment. The Battle of Dunkirk, on May 20, 1940, marked, he said, a turning point in history. The hope of creating a society in which each man, woman, and child would be relatively free from want and free to express their opinions was being shattered by the ominous specters of Nazism and Marxism and the growth of the munitions industry. The traditional humanistic values which had been the legacy of Roman civilization no longer seemed to have a place in the European world. In Picón's view the tragedy of war was the victimization of the individual and his creative spirit. Disillusioned with the European political scene, Picón now looked to the United States.[6] He saw the democratic institutions there as a counterpoise to Nazism, Communism, and Fascism. He compared the task of democracy to the function of literature. With democratic government there exists the possibility of man's institutions constantly renewing themselves. Democracy, he said, was similar to the flow of blood in human arteries: "Biologically a perfect democratic system can be compared with a good blood supply irrigating the body in which the work of the arteries always arrives at the heart. On the other hand, dictatorships in which all the functions of society are absorbed by the dictator soon die of historical embolism." [7] Yet Picon's view of the United States was not without criticism. Similar to many other Latin American writers, the Venezuelan essayist became anxious over the concentration in the United States on material progress. He deplored the exploitation of Latin America's natural resources by United States companies. Similar to José Enrique Rodó, he wondered whether or not the pragmatic sense of life in the United States was not antithetical to the spiritual concept of life found in the Latin American nations. At the same time Picón admired the Anglo-American work ethic which he thought Latin Americans should emulate. He sensed in the American working class a kind of fundamental heroism which contrasted with the false notion of heroism popularized by war. It was not heroic, said Picón, to destroy; it was heroic to create. It was heroic for men to develop the resources of the earth and to capitalize on their individual talents. In this kind of heroism, Picón saw a symbol of poetry and humility.

In one of the essays dealing with Franklin D. Roosevelt's "Good Neighbor Policy," Picón Salas saw the possibility for Latin America and the United States to resolve their differences on the basis of a fundamental sense of fraternal interdependence which all men must recognize.[8] He thought that both the United States and Latin America could profit from the cultural virtues which each had to offer to the world. Each nation or each culture had, as does a coin, an obverse-positive and reverse-negative side. The objective in life is to discover the positive values in men of different cultural backgrounds and to attempt to incorporate those values into one's own society. In this way, according to the author, the peoples of the world will, as they reach out to observe their neighbors, recognize the common humanity in all men.

In the essay entitled "Profecía de la palabra" ("Prophecy of the Word"), the essayist looks to the future of America and Europe with a sense of anticipation for what will happen after World War II is over.[9] He contended that one of the most important principles of life to remember is that man does not live by bread alone. Nations and political leaders must assist the people in developing a more spiritual sense of life in order to avoid future holocausts. Furthermore, nations must jettison the attitude of extreme nationalism which creates rivalries among different peoples. A more universal notion of politics would have to develop out of the ashes of war.

One particular issue which concerned Picón in "Profecía de la palabra" more than any other was the position of the intellectual in society. In the past, he noted, intellectuals had successfully divorced themselves from the reality of life and concentrated their efforts on aesthetic problems. Because of the war, it was no longer feasible for them to live out their lives in such a fashion; they had to become committed to the essential problems of the individual man. The world, Picón said, was at a crossroads. It had to choose between the development of a cultural pattern which enhanced the significance of the individual or one which saw the individual as a part of a collectivized whole. It was up to the intellectuals to see to it that government respected the rights of individuals. If they did not meet this obligation, Picón feared that after the end of the war the world would once again be ruled by the demogoguery of irrational men.

VIII *Venezuela*

In *Comprensión de Venezuela* (1948), Picón Salas examines his nation's cultural problems and the reasons why, in his opinion, Venezuela had not succeeded in establishing a sense of its cultural identity following independence from Spain. According to Picón, civilization is caught in a constant battle between the survival of humanistic cultural values and a dehumanization process generated through ignorance and the preeminence of material values over spiritual ones. Without humanistic values a

112   MARIANO PICÓN SALAS

nation cannot identify its mission in the world and, furthermore,
it has no way of relating its traditions to the present. He therefore
calls upon men of literature, historians, and educators to eradicate
incultura, loosely translated as the lack of culture. *Incultura,*
in Picón's essays, is the antithesis of *cultura,* or the acquisition of
cultural values. Venezuela in the nineteenth century experienced
two forms of cultural decadence: the decadence imposed by her
dictators, who succeeded in keeping the population ignorant and
illiterate, and the decadence of those writers who in the late
nineteenth century abandoned Venezuela for the literary salons
of Europe. The acquisition of an authentic cultural perspective
in a country is the result of a critical process in which men have
the opportunity to relate their creative talents to the particular
environment of that country and to the nation's traditions. For a
nation to possess a sense of its true culture it must be able to
establish an intellectual and emotional relationship between the
events of history and the land.

Cultura implies the capacity to grow. A sense of *cultura,* for
Picón Salas, is established in a country when that nation discovers its true identity within its traditions. For Venezuela to
achieve this goal it would be necessary for her educated class to
reinterpret the historical process beginning with the arrival of
the Spanish *conquistadores.* The objective of such a study had to
be the elimination of those negative historical ideas which had
kept the country from discovering the source of her vitality.

In *Comprensión de Venezuela,* Picón Salas structures his
search for the nation's cultural authenticity around the use of
three words: *patria, tierra,* and *cultura.* The word *patria,* or
fatherland, identifies the creation of a national myth of *venezolanidad. Tierra,* land, not only refers to the geographical limits
of the nation but encompasses the idea of a spiritual geography,
the particular topographical and climatic conditions which
determine, to some degree, the kind of society man will create.
Cultura, as already explained, identifies the spiritual and aesthetic
values which spring from tradition and the particular relationship
between man and his environment.

The initial essay of the book, entitled "Geografía con algunas
gentes" ("Geography and Some People"), is a physical description
of Venezuela in which the author relates the physical aspects of
the land to the political nature of the country and the entire cultural organism as a whole. For Picón, the irregular patterns of the

Venezuelan countryside identify the chaotic nature of Venezuelan politics beginning with the days following the Wars of Independence. The dictatorships of Cipriano Castro and Juan Vicente Gómez represent, as do the surface features of the land, the raw and undeveloped energy which had not been used for the benefit of all the people. The Venezuelan problem was that little had been done to channel the energy of the Venezuelan people into developing a productive sociopolitical structure. Though such a naturalistic interpretation of the political realities of the country appears deterministic, Picón mentions only that which had been factual in Venezuelan history. As we have already indicated, for Picón Salas, the essential ingredient in society is the will of the individual. In politics man has the potential for establishing any kind of political system he wants. Nineteenth-century historians assumed (an assumption with which the essayist strongly disagreed) that Venezuela was destined to live out its life under the control of *caudillos* and oppression. Picón, of course, rejected such negative views. His basic assumption was that *caudillo* rule through brute force did not represent a national characteristic. It was the result of misplaced energy and the abdication of responsibility on the part of the educated to form governments which would respect the integrity of the individual.

Picón believed that the authentic cultural identity of any given nation had to take into account the entire cultural development of the land from the time man first established an organized society. Only in this way can people fully understand their potential. His interpretations are not scientific. For the contemporary anthropologist and sociologist they prove interesting at best. Picón deals with Venezuelan reality from a poetic perspective. He seeks to identify through his intuition the spiritual reality of Venezuelan history.

In *Comprensión de Venezuela*, Picón Salas viewed the political geography of the country as the continuing fusion of disparate cultural elements from Spanish, European, and indigenous groups. Because of particular socioeconomic conditions, no given group of people was ever able to control the destiny of the entire country. While there did exist an aristocracy in Caracas in the nineteenth century, it did not succeed in determining the political structure of the country. As a result, according to Picón, there developed in Venezuela a sense of social democracy notwithstanding the proliferation of dictatorial regimes during the nineteenth and twen-

tieth centuries. Picón's interpretation is that there exists in
Venezuela the opportunity for true political democracy and unity
because of, and not in spite of, her past.

Picón feared, as did many of the Latin American writers of the
early twentieth century, that the industrialization process, which
was largely the result of economic adventurism on the part of
United States corporations and banks, would impose on Latin
America a way of life alien to the traditions of the past. The conflict in Picón's mind became all the more acute because he realized
that for Venezuela to take its place in the world it would have to
reject many of its past cultural attitudes toward life. However,
industrialization also appeared to provide the means for educating
the population and for improving the general quality of life for all
citizens. To resolve this dilemma Picón advocated the integration
of past cultural values with the needs of a machine age. The problem was how to accomplish this feat. Picón himself does not provide any particular way of going about the task. In the final
analysis all he could do was to point out, as critic, the negative
aspects of modernization, and hope that, through a revised educational system, people would come to sense the need to maintain a
spiritual sense of life. He believed that in order for Venezuelans
and other Latin Americans to maintain their spiritual integrity in
light of the economic transformation of the hemisphere, there had
to develop a deeper interest in the cultural heritage of the country.

Picón Salas interprets the path of Venezuelan history in terms
of a linear development leading from a sense of individualism
evident during the period of Conquest, to a sense of community
based on language and a common heritage which began with the
colonial period. In this interpretation Picón characterizes the
events of the nineteenth century as representing the cultural
pluralism of the nation and the struggle between rural and urban
centers in an attempt to unify the country. That this sought after
unity was not achieved is unimportant to Picón; the important
thing to know is that the struggle represented an attempt to
minimize the economic power of the aristocracy. The caudillos
were usually members of a rural peasant class. They failed because
of their perspective of history and politics. They did not see themselves as part of any tradition, but rather organized their rebellions
and governments considering only their own aggrandizment in
the present; they had no awareness of the future of the nation.

The colonial period, said Picón, cannot be interpreted as a mere period of exploitation. It must be considered a formative period, a period in which there developed a new concept of man and a noble debate concerning the universal concepts of freedom and human dignity. It was true that the Spanish soldiers raped the indigenous tribes of America. Yet out of the Conquest there did arise a new mestizo culture which sought the means for its own self-expression. In summary, Picón's views regarding the Conquest are best represented in the following quote dealing with Latin American independence: "The struggle for the Independence of America did not end in Ayacucho; it is a struggle which revives itself in each generation. And, as Benedetto Croce has stated in an admirable book, History would be a vain exercise in rhetoric about past deeds which are irreversible if man did not see in them a permanent struggle toward liberty." [10]

In the essay entitled *Paseo por nuestra poesía* (*A Stroll through Our Poetry*), Picón Salas dealt with the idea of cultural authenticity which he compares to literary authenticity. He interprets literary authenticity as a coalescing between subject and literary form. Cultural authenticity must be interpreted in a similar way. In the first place, it is not to be confused with the mere expression of regional mores. Nor is it a nostalgic desire to recreate traditions which are no longer relevant. It is, however, the process by which the people make use of new forms of technology to fit their own needs. It is the process, gained through education, by which the people go about the task of developing *cultura*. In the twentieth century the cultural task was to transform the nation into a modern state. In order for Venezuela to establish a sense of its own cultural authenticity, Picón Salas stated that it was necessary for the nation to reach out into the world at large and abstract from that world those elements which would be beneficial in perfecting the Venezuelan attitude toward life. As well as incorporating views from without, Picón Salas stated that is would be necessary for the nation to unify itself once and for all.

Sociologically, said Picón, Venezuela after the civil wars of the nineteenth century was like a political mountain range, clusters of small hills without a central administration to guide its destiny. It was a country in which only the strongest and most cunning could attempt to impose their rule. In such a milieu, it was impossible, therefore, for a sense of cultural authenticity to develop. Venezuela, in the nineteenth century, was like an enormous novel about people who had no specific direction, who simply threw them-

selves into following what appeared to be most advantageous.
There existed no sense of cultural solidarity. Revolutions seemed
to have been created because there was nothing better to do.
Furthermore, with no well established educational system, the
country lived under a veil of ignorance. For those who were educated, the notion of culture did not spring from their roots—it
was a notion which developed as a way of avoiding anything
typically Venezuelan. There was a literature but the subject of
that literature only had a snob appeal. It was not directed to the
country. It sought a sense of spiritual and intellectual salvation in
European culture. The only quasi-redeeming factor in this literature was that it did recapture some of the folklore of Venezuelan
culture. However, the only reason that writers were interested in
writing this literature was for its exotic appeal. It was a literature
of escapism.

In the final two essays of the book, "Notas sobre el problema de
nuestra cultura" ("Notes on the Problem of Our Culture") and
"Auditorio de juventud" ("An Audience of Youth"), Picón reiter-
ates some of the problems already mentioned. He seeks to offer
suggestions to younger generations for a way to approach the subjects of cultural authenticity and the future of the nation. The first
thing that had to happen in Venezuela was the development of a
philosophical orientation of society through education. This orientation would establish an atmosphere of willingness to deliberate
over historical and political problems. In the past, Venezuela had
become accustomed to following the law and order of dictators.
Now it was necessary to reprogram the nation's youth to think for
themselves. It was also up to the leaders of the country to perpetuate a critical climate without which democracy could not be
established. Under the dictators society was divided into two
groups: the good who adhered to the rule of the dictator, and the
bad who opposed him. The philosophy of government had been
reduced to a kind of pragmatism fitted to suit the psychological
orientation of the caudillo. Picón believed that the historical
process could be reversed once the nation decided that it was going to integrate its many disparate social and economic elements.
Venezuela had to permit what the essayist called a civilizing
process to take place. It had to develop a new civilization brought
about by uniting towns with new roads, one which would recognize the aesthetic and moral values inherent in rural life, which

would permit each section of the country to maintain its individual identity, and that would not require people to leave the land
but realize the interdependence between man and the soil he
works.

CHAPTER 7

A Search for Paradise Lost

I *Paradise Lost*

MARIANO Picón Salas' *Viaje al amanecer*, a series of personal recollections of life in Mérida, is a search for paradise lost, cultural authenticity, an identity. The journey toward the center of existence, is an attempt to recreate through literature the fond memories of the author's childhood in the foothills of the Andes mountains. Juxtaposed alongside life's realities, the vision in *Viaje al amanecer* is utopian. Mariano Picón Salas sets out in his work to regain a sense of the spiritual essence of provincial life and to reestablish the fundamental psychological and cultural identity of his own being.

The theme of *errancia*, or peregrination, evident in the title of *Viaje al amanecer*, is both an emotional and spiritual return to the beginning of the author's existence. *Errancia*, as return, completes the circular design of the author's voyages and adventures. *Viaje al amanecer* crystallizes the aesthetic dimension of the author's desire to identify his intellectual *errancia* as a fundamental search for personal identity. It may be said that the direction of peregrination in this book is a reversal of the essayist's earlier attempts to challenge the world with his idealism. If *Buscando el camino* demonstrates a spirit of adventure in pursuit of the multifarious forms of reality, *Viaje al amanecer* illustrates the underlying nostalgia that accompanied the writer in his travels away from Venezuela.

Viaje al amanecer is a reaction to a debilitating world economic and spiritual crisis. In the technological age, Picón saw man reducing his vision to systematic calculations. *Viaje al amanecer* rediscovers mysteries and uncertainties in the legends and traditions of Mérida life. The author reconstructs a period of his own life when reality and idealism, history and legend, and truth and fantasy seemed indistinguishable from each other. In Mérida, there existed two visions of life, which Picón defined as *fantasía bárbara* and *fantasía culta* (uncultured and cultured imagination).[1] Picón Salas saw in Mérida the existence of a total and authentic vision of life. Scientific and intuitive knowledge became integrated into the provincial vision of the world: a unique blend, for Picón, of subjective and objective truths, a form of intellectual and emotional utopia.

In the poetic world of Mérida, Picón identified the spiritual relationship between man and his environment. Part of the mythological world of Mérida is referred to as "la geografía del aire" ("the geography of the air"). As a young boy, the author learned about the geography of the air filled with signs and messages, which most men are not able to interpret, from an illiterate farmer and friend, Rafael.[2] Born on the slopes of the Andes mountains, where he spent all his life, Rafael conveyed to the young Picón an intuitive and poetic sense of the drama in nature. Rafael's knowledge about the birds, the land, the mountains, and the clouds was born out of observation and close contact with nature. His interpretation of life is an untutored awareness of reality, an example of *fantasía bárbara*: "And in order to foretell the changes in the weather, that which was going to happen, nothing more necessary was needed than that science of prediction through symbols. Rafael, who grew up in the mountains, who became accustomed to looking at the sky as if it were a mirror, who imitated the call of different birds and the sound of some animal about to devour the chickens, told me all about his extraordinary world." [3] The things or *cosas* that Rafael knows are identified in the lessons given to his young friend as a philosophy, or religion, of nature. Rafael's *fantasía bárbara* is pantheistic, combining empirical observation with Catholic cosmology. For example, in the flock of birds that circles over the valley at the end of October, Rafael sees the flight of penitent souls: "They are the penitent souls which did not have the opportunity of repenting before dying. They return, when All Souls Day draws near, to see if a responsorial prayer or flask of holy water will improve their condition." [4] Opposed to *fantasía bárbara* is the *fantasía culta* of the educated classes in Mérida, which recognized that provincial traditions would soon succumb to modernity.

The voyage in *Viaje al amanecer* leads the reader from the essayist's search for universal values—a sense of history, art, and culture—to contemplate the particular circumstances and value structure of provincial life. I stated earlier that the concept of the universal in Picón Salas does not negate the existence of the particular. So, too, in *Viaje al amanecer* the particular does not invalidate the importance of incorporating universal values into provincial life. As Picón stated in 1941, Venezuela had to develop a collective national psychology in which each segment, or cultural region, would contribute to the formation of the country's collective soul.[5] The particular—in this case *patria chica*—subsumes the existence of a universal—*patria*, or Venezuela. Picón, consciously or unconsciously, illustrates the legendary history of the nation as a whole in his descriptions of the particularity of life in Mérida.

The provincial element in *Viaje al amanecer* establishes an intimate relationship between the author's personal search for identity and the cultural identity of a particular circumstance. For Picón Salas, the preservation of individual identity superseded all other considerations. In *1941: Cinco discursos sobre pasado y presente de la nación venezolana, (1941: Five Lectures on Past and Present of Venezuelan Culture)*, he stated the importance of each state to maintain and preserve its cultural identity while, at the same time, attempting to incorporate into the body politic the universal concepts of democracy. Democracy was important to Picón Salas, for without it the individual in society had little chance to discover the autonomy of self. Nevertheless, Picón—always concerned with the question of identity—saw the primordial function of the state as consisting in the maintainence and preservation of the spirit of its particular heritage. The provincial quality of *Viaje al amanecer* points to the author's preoccupation with the preservation of individual existence. The return in *Viaje al amanecer* unites the author's search for personal identity with that of *patria chica*. In this book, Picon identified himself as a *merideño entrañable* ("a Meridean body and soul").[6]

Picón's ambivalence toward change appears as a dichotomy between a concept of tradition as static (*tradición estática*) and a concept of tradition as dynamic (*tradición dinámica*).[7] Tradition as static had a negative value for the essayist; it represented the vision of those who regretted, at each juncture in time, the eclipsing of outmoded traditions which had kept the country in a state of political and economic underdevelopment. In developing a concept of tradition as dynamic, Picón Salas sought to oppose the

former with a more critical attitude toward traditions. He interpreted the concept of *tradición dinámica* as a fusion between the
idea of history as change and history as continuity. In *Viaje al
amanecer*, there exist both a nostalgic sense of continuity and an
awareness that Mérida must incorporate itself into the larger
cultural entity of Venezuela through technological change. This
dualism becomes apparent in the author's struggle to harmonize
his emotional attachment to the valley with an awareness that the
process of regional growth, as in the development of the individual, necessitates the introduction of new social and economic
modalities. The myth of Maricastaña (see section II of this chapter) provides the connection, or sense of continuity, between the
present and a period of time that preceded the author's own
existence. The book, at the same time, traces the forward trajectory of the author's life up to the time when it was necessary
for him to leave the province for Caracas. The structure of *Viaje al
amanecer* is a peregrination of the author's emergence from youth
to adolescence and from dreams to reality. The recreation of
scenes of youth and the legends that structured the author's early
awareness of life represents a lyrical continuity which the author
wanted to preserve. The element of change, on the other hand—
change is the essence of *errancia*—is made clear in the final chapter of the book in which we see the young Picón preparing to leave
the valley. The act of leaving symbolizes a transition, a frontier of
change which trancends the personal significance of the author's
voyage: "We crossed a new frontier. We arrived with anticipation
in the new district. In front of us, similar to the blue and distant
ridge of the *cordillera* for the traveler, there appeared a diffused
outline of the things to come and the people we would meet." [8]

II *Paradise Regained*

In *Viaje al amanecer*, Maricastaña, the goddess of time, is transformed into the muse of Picón Salas' recollections.[9] As time personified, Maricastaña helps the author to bridge the gap between his
memories and the present. Picón Salas describes her as an old
woman wearing glasses, hunched over a spinning wheel, reeling
out the thread of time and destiny: "Maricastaña, who was prob-
ably an old woman with glasses, bent over her spinning wheel,
spinning out not only the white thread, but the destiny of all men
as well." [10] The myth of Maricastaña symbolizes the dawn of the

author's awakening to the reality of life in the provinces and the
connection between his own life and that of those who lived before him: "It was the myth of my youth, of the things and the
people who preceded me in life; a symbol which united all my
ancestors with the young boy of four that I was and who one day
awoke surprised to learn that he had grown up in the society of
all those people." [11] Maricastaña represented an illusion of the past
as the youth fantasized how things must have been before he was
born. The myth of Maricastaña enabled Picón to idealize the lives
of the members of his family. The history of Venezuela transformed
into legend as he learned from his elders about the wars, the earth-
quakes, the apparitions of the supernatural world, and the peregrination of his forefathers who came to settle in Mérida to find
peace and tranquillity: "The history of Mérida, all that had occurred in the vast land mass of Venezuela, the wars, the earth-
quakes, the apparitions of the devil—the protagonist of many
legends in Mérida—were, for me, located in an imaginative notion
of the past which was precisely the period when Maricastaña
lived." [12]

The search for paradise lost contains within itself its own source
of disillusionment. The search for paradise lost can only exist as
nostalgia and a temporary literary retreat from reality. Just as in
the story about the town undertaker, Apolinar Gaviria, the treasure of paradise lost resides only in the imagination of the author.
Apolinar Gaviria, as related by Picón, set as the goal of his life the
discovery of a treasure, which, according to legend, rested in some
unknown place in the valley of Mérida. After years of unprofitable
search, Apolinar Gaviria developed a theory to explain his failure
to discover the treasure. Similar to the geophysical ideas of the
movement of continents, Apolinar Gaviria proclaimed that the
land in Mérida was in a constant state of motion, thereby preclud-
ing his discovery of the treasure. Yet, he continued to hope that
by chance the treasure would still be found. The difficulty in re-
discovering the treasure of paradise lost, for Picón Salas, was that
the forces of change in the twentieth century were quickly restruc-
turing the society throughout the continent.

Historically, as stated by the author, Mérida represented an
oasis of repose. For the Spanish conquistadors, the valley was a
retreat from their peregrination and the search for fortune. Mérida
was viewed, by the conquistadors, as an ideal setting in the diaphanous quality of its mountain air and its cool running streams. It

was a land to remain in and it beckoned the termination of their voyage: "Era tierra para quedarse y no para continuar errando" ("It was a land to settle down in and not for continuing one's peregrination").[13]

Mérida then is perfection, a Garden of Eden. Picón returns to his native land with a sense of contrition for the cultural distance created between his own intellectual development and the serenity of provincial life. Earlier, he was anxious to leave the influence that religion held in the lives of the people. At that time Mérida represented a limitation to his further awareness of the world. In *Viaje al amanecer* he seeks indulgence, as a penitent, from the people and the institutions that he left behind when he set out to challenge the world. Hopeful of reincorporating the spiritual life of the valley into his own spirit, he begs forgiveness and wishes that he will one day be buried in the sacred ground of the cemetery of Santa Juana: "I hope that the venerable chapel of the cathedral has exonerated me from the charge of heretic with which I was labeled and, like the elders I knew, I will be permitted burial in the colonial cemetary of Santa Juana, where the lime of the bodies of those who lay there produced the sweetest and most brilliantly colored oranges." [14]

Mérida is harmony. The natural elements of the country, its streams, its plants and creatures all interact to produce a vision of an Arcadia reminiscent of the pastoral. In the *llanos*, life is brutal; nature is hostile toward man. In Mérida the natural elements synchronize their movements to produce a poetic symphony:

> The cold waters which descend from the snow capped mountains; the trees with their shiny green leaves and their peaceful shade; the ferns and the moss which crystallize with the dew, the eternal rumbling of the four white and foamy streams which bathe the base of Mérida's plateaus; the constant flight of birds of many varieties in the polished blue sky, the sierra region with its cold peaks called Toro, Columna, León, serving as an enormous backdrop which Nature erected, gave to my city a special sense of delight in comparison to Venezuela's other cities.[15]

In Mérida the past, providing the inhabitants with a romantic awareness of their *infra-historia*, blends into the present through its traditions and oral history. The dead do not die in the valley; their spirit lives and mythicizes their deeds. As stated in Picón, time is stratified in Mérida. The present is filled with the meaning of the past and the inhabitants travel between past and present almost as if past and present were one. In reality, the past is superimposed on the present. But, for Picón Salas, the concept of time—stratified—opposes the horizontal perception of time in the city where traditions are not revered. City men react neurotically to time for they fear the loss of the present. In order to compensate for the present's fleeting characteristic, city men strive to fill their lives with activities designed to stimulate only a sensory response to life: "Time for him who is born in Mérida is dense and stratified —so different from the nervous sense of time which has the tendency to forget, such as is lived in more modern cities. The past blends in with the present and people who lived three centuries ago or who lived only in the fearful imagination of the people of Mérida were ever present in our daily lives." [16] In Mérida, the urge to consume the present does not exist. When death comes to the individual in the valley, there springs forth the desire to integrate the spirit with the souls of those who populated the country in earlier generations. Death, then, represents an eternity in the infrahistory of the valley.

Life in Mérida is spiritual. The social and cultural activities of the inhabitants are circumscribed by a religious interpretation of life. In the spiritual concepts of the people there exists a unity between the passage of the year according to the ecclesiastical calendar and the natural cycle in the change of seasons. As a Latin American village, Mérida is not unique. The reality of religion is fundamental to all of Latin American society. Furthermore, anthropological studies see an intimate relationship between religious ceremony and social activity in nearly all rural and sedentary communities. In Picón Salas the role of religion in Mérida contrasts, as in his examination of other cultural phenomena, with the lack of spiritual life in the city. Even though religion has not vanished from the city, the quest for material comfort has mitigated its importance. In the city, the days of the week and the months of the year have acquired only a numerical value as men go about the task of increasing their wealth. For Picón Salas, the ceremonial function of religion provides a sense of meaning that transcends the passage of time as linear or horizontal. The particular interaction between spiritual beliefs, social activity, and natural phenomena provides a sense of authenticity that individualizes a community from other communities. The author's concept of *venezolanidad* is, precisely, a quest for the spiritual identity of his people. In Picón Salas, religion is important for its cultural value. He is not concerned with dogma, or the truths that religion attempts to establish. Religion is a reality, a reality which Picón Salas saw as a human need.

In Mérida the tedium of life was broken by the ritualistic passage of the year. From January to December, the calendar provided a sense of hope and an interpretation of human suffering as an act of penance in preparation for the eternal meeting with God: "In order to count the passage of time and to add color to the months of the year, without which they would pass in a monotonous way, there are many Church feast days. Over the twelve houses of the year were erected the flowered monuments of saints along with the flame from candles made from the wax which the bees of Mérida fabricate with ecclesiastical diligence." [17]

Viaje al amanecer is Picon Salas' lyrical recommitment to the vision of life and principles first expressed in *Buscando el camino*. Here Picón urged writers to seek out man's humility and sincerity in relationships between the individual and the community. Unlike Carlyle, who searched for the identity of heroes, Picón thought that history should pay greater tribute to men who expressed the Christian virtues—love, simplicity, and humility—in their actions and interactions with others. Man's spiritual condition was, for Picón Salas, represented in the tiller's affection for the soil and his family: "One must discover man, man who seeks to live in the furrows of the land and who sweats from working the land, in the house in the country where he lives with his wife and children and where he drinks his beer and smokes his pipe on feast days; man who does not have to be a hero because he aspires mainly to be able to produce a good harvest and be like other men in his work and in love." [18]

In *Viaje al amanecer* the author reconstructed the simplicity of life in Mérida. In the marketplace, in the processions that mark holy days, at weddings and funerals, there are no heroes. *Viaje al amanecer* is a recollection of family and friends: Rafael, Pablo Riolid, Picón's grandfather; Monsieur Machy, intellectual and skeptic; Josefita, the idealized and romantic visionary of historical events; Apolinar Gaviria, undertaker; the *beata*; Eulogio, teacher; María Eudocia, who interpreted Halley's comet in 1910 as a sign of the coming of the Antichrist and the destruction of the world. Picón's reintegration into the spiritual and cultural life in Mérida is a reaction against world chaos. Maricastaña, representing nostalgia and hope of recapturing the essence of paradise lost, acts as a substitute figure for the Antichrist in the world. Picón describes life in the valley in the style of the nineteenth-century *costumbristas*, who wrote about mores and customs. His purpose, however, transcends description for its own sake. The author's rediscovery of the valley's spritual life is less a retreat from the world than a statement of the need to reestablish a sense of Christian cultural values and the spiritual aspect of tradition.

CHAPTER 8

Conclusion

THE work of Mariano Picón Salas illustrates the internal struggle of twentieth-century Latin American writers to discover the cultural authenticity and identity of their respective countries and the continent in general. The essential problem, particularly at the turn of the century and after modernism, was whether to consider the development of the hemisphere in terms of the cultural manifestations within individual countries or to consider each country as a manifestation of a more general hemispheric development.[1] The resolution to the problem had to be found in defining the particular reality as an expression of the universal. In general, the Latin American essayists divided into two camps: those who, perceiving dictatorship as inevitable and part of the organic structure of each country and society, subscribed to the concepts of cultural fatalism, and those who, determining that Latin Americans could, through the exercise of their will, overcome the legacy of *caudillismo* and the rigidity of traditionalism, envisioned a more positive future for the continent. Together with José Vasconcelos, Pedro Henríquez-Ureña, Alfonso Reyes, and others, Mariano Picón Salas supported the contention that Latin America, with its mestizo culture, held out the promise of becoming the utopia envisioned by the first Spanish conquerors.

Picón Salas' particular circumstance was Venezuela, and, more particularly, the province of Mérida where the author was born. Both Mérida and Venezuela provided the author with a sense of cultural identity which he felt necessary to define and redefine throughout his essays, notwithstanding the years of self-exile and travel spent away from his homeland.

As an essayist Picón Salas interpreted his genre to be a bridge between poetry and philosophy. The essayist's function, he said, was to assist in guiding man out of the labyrinth of life's struggles. He did not see the essayist as providing man with a systematic approach to life. Picón was not an ideologue. Philosophical systems, however well-intentioned, have a tendency of becoming rigid in their approach to human problems. In their ultimate dogmatism, systems, or ideologies, they fail to recognize the effects of historical and social change on the systems themselves. For this reason, Picón Salas opposed the Marxian approach to resolving the economic and political difficulties that faced, and still face, the Latin American countries. The essayist's function should be directive, so as to provide a form for man's passions. Picón saw life as a dialectical struggle between reason and passion.

Mariano Picón Salas was an idealist. Venezuela's history had exemplified the polarization of vested interests and the personal, arbitrary rule of the caudillo. Yet, Picón discovered in Francisco de Miranda, Andrés Bello, and Simón Bolívar cultural ideals which, for the author, represented a fundamental cultural idealism in the nation's personality. In his search for the country's spiritual essence, or *venezolanidad*, Picón sought to resurrect the concepts of Hispanic Americanism that showed these men to be leaders of universal importance. Largely influenced by Bello, Picón hoped to create a politics of culture ("una política de cultura").[2] In 1941, the essayist addressed a group of university students. He urged the younger generation of Venezuelans to erect through culture— an aesthetic and ethical ideal—a human ideal that would inspire all Venezuelans to develop a superior national spirit. He said: "To establish a more responsible and creative human ideal than that of the cheap mediocrity which for many years has turned to stone our collective existence seems to me to be a duty for a younger generation. One of the ways to arrive at such a goal is through culture." [3] Although Picón's address was primarily designed to stimulate an interest in Venezuela's national heritage, I can state that the goals sought for the country were also those he desired for all mankind. Picón Salas, in his particularism, was constantly in search of universal principles and harmony between all men. Similar to Teilhard de Chardin, the author sought to develop a cosmic awareness of reality ("una conciencia cósmica").[4]

In Venezuela, Picón Salas was an innovator. Unlike many of the essayists and historians who preceded him, Picón sought to synthesize the struggles that had created the polarization between social classes and between the two concepts of Venezuelan nationhood that had been created by the caudillos from within and by political exiles living elsewhere. He tried to demonstrate that

Venezuela was a product of a rich colonial heritage and that that heritage had its roots in the history of Western civilization.

Picón saw the hope of a better society in the spiritual and intellectual development of the individual. His answer to the political conflicts of the day was to educate the individual to a universal awareness of culture and ethics. Among Picón's major concerns was the relationship between ethics and aesthetics. He sought to inject a sense of obligation to nation in the aesthetic forms created by the Latin American and Venezuelan modernists. His literary search was a quest for the proper form to express self-identity and the authenticity of *venezolanidad*. Picón sought harmony between form and content, as applied to literature and to life itself. For Picón *patria* and cultural heritage were forms that contained the spirit and passion of man. In order to achieve self-expression leading to the development of the individual's spiritual personality, Picón thought that the individual had first to submit to the cultural forms evident in the reality of circumstance. Like other Latin Americans of his generation, Picón was influenced by Bergson's intuitionism. In his essays, intuitionism represents a faith in the writer as a spiritual being. Intuitionism, as a means of interpreting history, is a reaction to scientific determinism, which in the nineteenth century was only concerned with society's organic structure. Picón's intuitionism represented faith in the continent's potential and progress.

Notwithstanding his affinity for rural life and the simplicity represented in the *campesinos*' life-style, Picón did not really write for the masses. He was an intellectual who remained aloof from the world of politics. In fact he feared revolution as the substitution of one form of tyranny for another. Picón sought the liberation of men's minds from the turmoil and boredom of daily existence and from the effects of political propaganda. The essential problem in life was not between the haves and the have-nots, but between being and possessing. In being man discovered the nature of his spiritual identity; in possessing man subjugated himself to material riches and lost the power to be.

Picón saw himself as an intellectual, a wandering bohemian, in search of a way to establish his own identity and to pursue that identity in the formation of a spiritual self. His peregrination through life was an endless quest for ideals and essence. Picón Salas was a romantic in search of life's mysteries. In his travels to Brazil, Chile, Mexico, and Peru, he sought to uncover what he called the continent's cosmic mystery ("misterio cósmico"). Picón described the nature of his peregrination, or *errancia*, as he called it, as follows: "To travel through America is to come in contact with this mystery, to listen to the clamoring of the people, to know both the refined aspects of its society and its barbarism, to hear the voice of reason and that of passion, and to experience that primordial urge of wanting to be." [5]

My study has focused in on Picón Salas' peregrination, or *errancia*—Picon's neologism for peregrination—between 1920 and 1941. The *errancia* traced in previous chapters is both Picon's physical voyage away from Mérida to Chile and his intellectual peregrination in pursuit of identity and utopia. I have hoped to demonstrate the particular relationship between internal and external reality and how these realities joined in the formation of the author's total vision of life.

Notes and References

Chapter One

1. John Edwin Fagg, *Latin America, a General History* (London, 1969), p. 616.

2. See Laureano Vallenilla Lanz, *Disgregación e integración*, for a positivist interpretation of Venezuelan history. For the most part, the positivist historian held a negative view of the nineteenth century and the possibilities for progress in Venezuela. His view of history was organic and attributed the disunity and violence of the century to the physical structure of society. Vallenilla Lanz was an apologist for the caudillo regime of Juan Vicente Gómez. He supported Gómez on the grounds that the Venezuelan people could not decide their destiny within a democratic structure of government. According to Vallenilla Lanz, the Venezuelan people possessed a weakness of character and, therefore, they needed a paternalistic leader to guide them.

3. Carlos Irazábal, *Venezuela, esclava y feudal* (Caracas, 1964), pp. 59–66. The interpretation of Venezuelan history by Irazábal represents a more positive view of the country's capacity to overcome the chaos of the nineteenth century. Similar to the basic concept of Mariano Picón Salas, Irazábal does not view the events of history as inevitable. The civil strife of the nineteenth century was due to socio-economic conditions which could be corrected. The essential problem of the nineteenth century was that the colonial economic system, which was feudalistic, did not change radically with political independence. Although the leaders of independence sought to establish a republican form of government, they failed to recognize the relationship between political ideals and economic realities.

4. George S. Wise, *Antonio Guzmán Blanco: A Study of Caudillismo* (Ann Arbor, 1950), p. 9.

5. Fagg, *Latin America, a General History*, p. 617.

6. For an in-depth analysis of foreign economic influence in Venezuela at the turn of the century and after, read Frederico Brito Figueroa's *Venezuela, siglo XX* (Havana, 1967). The general interpretation of historical events and of the United States influence in

Venezuela is Marxist. Brito Figueroa's study presents many graphs and figures to sustain his argument of United States economic imperialism. While some may contest the conclusions found in this book, the essential value of the work is in the historical completeness with which the author argues his position.

7. See José Enrique Rodó's *Ariel* for an understanding of the position of many Latin American intellectuals with regard to the increasing influence of the United States in Latin America at the turn of the century. The phrase "colossus of the north" is an ominous metaphor for Latin American essayists. Inherent in the phrase is the fear that the northern giant will, eventually, dominate the life of the smaller and weaker Spanish American republics.

8. Particular attention should be paid to the following works: Pedro Henríquez Ureña, *Seis ensayos en busca de nuestra expresión* and *Historia de la cultura en la América Hispánica;* José Carlos Mariátegui, *Seite ensayos en busca de la realidad peruana;* Mariano Picón Salas, *De la conquista a la independencia. Tres siglos de historia cultural;* Alfonso Reyes, *Simpatías y diferencias* and *Visión de anahuac;* José Enrique Rodó, *Ariel;* José Vasconcelos, *Ulísis criollo.*

9. One of the first Latin American essayists to formulate a theory of social and moral harmony in the continent was the Puerto Rican writer Eugenio María de Hostos (1839–1903). Hostos was, essentially, a positivist influenced by the English essayist Herbert Spencer. Hostos conceived of the existence of a natural, individual, and social morality. Important to the writers of the twentieth century was the Puerto Rican essayist's concept of "eurítmia social." Inherent in the phrase is an aesthetic perception of the social order. The essayists of the twentieth century relied heavily on intuition and the search for metaphysical values in their attempt to bring social and political harmony to the continent.

10. Culturally speaking, the dilemma that I allude to is the idea of the twentieth-century essayists that Latin America did not possess an awareness of its cultural and historical identity. The political dilemma referred to is the instability of Latin American governments and the difficulties in setting up a democratic political system.

11. "Pequeña confesión a la sordina," *Obras selectas* (Caracas, 1966), p. xiv. The remainder of the quotations taken from the *Obras selectas* shall be from this edition.

12. José Ramón Medina, *50 años de literatura venezolana* (Caracas, 1969), p. 186.

13. Guillermo Korn, "Del positivismo al modernismo en la prensa venezolana," *Historia de la cultura en Venezuela* (Caracas, 1956), II, 54.

14. Ibid., p. 57.

15. Luis Beltrán Guerrero, "Introducción al positivismo venezolano," in *Historia de la cultura en Venezuela* (Caracas, 1956), II, 199–233.

16. Ibid.

17. See Rafael Villavicencia, *La evolución*.

18. José Ramón Medina, *50 años de literatura venezolana* (Caracas, 1969), p. 15.

19. Arturo Uslar Pietri, "El milagro de la poesía," *El Nacional*, July 20, 1954. This article is also cited in the literary history by José Ramón Medina.

20. See Henri Louis Bergson, *Oeuvres* (Paris, 1959), for an understanding of the relationship between the immediate circumstances of life and individual awareness.

21. Angel Rosenblat, "Lengua y cultura de Venezuela," in *Historia de la cultura en Venezuela* (Caracas, 1956), II, 83.

22. Rafael Angarita Arvelo, "La crítica literaria en Venezuela," *Revista Nacional de Cultura*, 16, no. 105 (1954), 13.

23. A partial list of the more important works on Rómulo Gallegos is as follows. Within Venezuela: Angel Damboriena, *Rómulo Gallegos y la problemática venezolana* (Caracas, 1960); Orlando Araujo, *Lengua y creación en la obra de Rómulo Gallegos* (Caracas, 1962); Felipe Massiani, *El hombre y la naturaleza en Rómulo Gallegos* (Caracas, 1964); Pedro Díaz Seijas, *Rómulo Gallegos, realidad y símbolo* (Caracas, 1965). Outside of Venezuela: Leo Ulrich, *Rómulo Gallegos: estudio sobre el arte de novelar* (Mexico City, 1954); Lowell Dunham, *Rómulo Gallegos*, translated into Spanish by the Venezuelan writer and politician Gonzalo Barrios and Ricardo Montilla, as *Rómulo Gallegos; vida y obra* (Mexico City, 1957).

24. Luis Alberto Sánchez, *Nueva historia de la literatura americana* (Buenos Aires, 1949), pp. 180–85.

25. Domingo Miliani, *Vida intelectual en Venezuela* (Caracas, 1971), p. 137.

26. *Literatura venezolana* (Mexico City, 1945), p. 5.

27. Ibid., p. 7.

Chapter Two

1. Ad Stender-Petersen, "Esquisse d'une theorie structurale de la litterature," *Recherches Structurales*, 5 (1949), 277–87. This article is also cited in James Willis Robb's *El estilo de Alfonso Reyes* (Mexico City, 1965).

2. José Luis Martínez, *El ensayo mexicano moderno* (Mexico City, 1958), p. 8.

3. Robert Mead, *Breve historia del ensayo hispanoamericano* (Mexico City, 1956), p. 8.

4. Carlos Ripoll, *Conciencia intelectual de América* (New York, 1966), p. 24.

5. Antonio de la Nuez, "Antiguos y nuevos metodos de penetración del ensayo," *Annuario de filología (la Universidad de Zulia)* (Maracaibo), No. 4. (n.d.)), 10.

6. Mariano Picón Salas, "En torno al ensayo," in *Cuadernos del congreso por la libertad de la cultura* (Paris, 1954), p. 32.

7. Ibid., p. 33.

8. "Literatura y sociedad," in *Hora y deshora* (Caracas, 1963), p. 52.

9. "En torno al ensayo," p. 33.

10. "Todavía Sarmiento," in *Hora y deshora* (Caracas, 1963), p. 77.

11. "En torno al ensayo," p. 33.

12. Ibid., p. 32.

13. *Comprensión de Venezuela* (Caracas, 1949), p. 8.

14. Ibid., p. 128.

15. Ibid., p. 9

16. "Literatura y sociedad," p. 51.

17. Ibid., p. 52.

18. Ibid., p. 51.

19. *Buscando el camino* (Caracas, 1920), p. 146.

20. "Testimonio de Gabriela," in *Hora y deshora* (Caracas, 1963), p. 105.

21. Picón Salas, *Comprensión de Venezuela*, p. 7. In the last part of this quotation, the author is referring to the fact that he remained aloof from politics. Because of his attitude toward political parties and propaganda he was accused of being a political conservative by elements of Venezuela's left-wing groups.

22. Ibid.

23. *Odisea de tierra firme* (Santiago, 1940), p. 15.

24. *Comprensión de Venezuela*, p. 81

25. "Visita a los malos salvajes," in *Los malos salvajes* (Buenos Aires, 1963), p. 40.

26. "Regreso y promisión," in *Regreso de tres mundos* (Mexico City, 1959), p. 111.

27. Pedro Emilio Coll, *La escondida senda* (Madrid, 1927), p. 18.

28. "Pequeña confesión a la sordina," in *Obras Selectas*, p. ix; this essay will hereafter be cited in the text as *P*.

29. Jurgen Hahn, *The Origins of the Baroque Concept of Peregrinatio* (Chapel Hill, 1973), p. 154.

Hahn traces the development of the concept of *peregrinatio* from the fifteenth century to the nineteenth century. He discovers a process that began with an external search for utopia and which eventually internalized in the discovery of self. In the fifteenth century the term pilgrimage, or *peregrinatio,* involved a religious search for the paradise that men lost due to original sin. The pilgrimages that were popular during the fifteenth century, according to Hahn, were manifestations of a dissatisfaction with the world as it was. There existed a need to rediscover the period of innocence before the fall of Adam and Eve.

The second aspect of *peregrinatio* developed in the nineteenth century with the romantic poets. The quest for a mystical reality became a psychological search for self-improvement and identity. As with the poet Lord Byron, the idea that prevailed in the nineteenth century was that external society had been responsible for divorcing the identity of the individual from the self. When the English poet insisted on visiting the ruins of antiquity in Rome, he did so in order to purge himself from the cultural accoutrements of Victorian English society. Byron attempted to find a way to reintegrate himself with an external concept of historical identity.

Both forms of *peregrinatio* contain the element of reintegration. In the fifteenth century the reintegrative process developed as a search for spiritual salvation. In the nineteenth century the reintegration of identity with self was a search for personal and psychological salvation.

30. "Adolescencia," in *Regreso de tres mundos* (Mexico City, 1959), p. 22.

31. *Los malos salvajes*, p. 10.

32. Manuel Díaz Rodríguez, *Camino de perfección* (Buenos Aires, 1908), p. 30.

33. *Buscando el camino*, p. 8.

34. "Artes, hombres," in *Buscando el camino* (Caracas, 1920), p. 30.

35. Ibid., p. 29

36. "La finalidad poco americana de una literatura," in *Buscando el camino* (Caracas, 1920), p. 137.

37. "Artes, hombres," p. 28.

38. *Buscando el camino*, p. 8.

39. "Vidas" in *Buscando el camino*, p. 17.

40. "Pintura de un vivir," in *Buscando el camino*, p. 125.

41. Picón Salas, *Mundo imaginario* (Santiago, 1927), p. 93.

42. Ernesto Mayz Vallenilla, *El problema de América* (Caracas, 1959), p. 16. Mayz Vallenilla defined the difference between *conciencia* and *conciencia de*. According to Mayz Vallenilla, Latin America did not need conscience. Conscience is a permanent condition. What was wanting in America was an awareness of reality (a *conciencia de*).

Chapter Three

1. See Miguel de Unamuno's essay "Adentro" for a further explanation of the meaning of *infra-historia*.

2. Alfonso Reyes, "Ultima Tule," *Obras completas,* XI (Mexico, 1960), p. 63.

3. *Literatura venezolana,* p. 11

4. "Adolescencia," in *Obras selectas,* p. 1338.

5. "Colecciono estas prosas," in *Buscando el camino* (Caracas, 1920), p. 8.

6. "Pintura de un vivir," in *Buscando el camino,* p. 124.

7. Ibid., p. 129.

8. "La finalidad poco americana de una literatura," in *Buscando el camino,* p. 148.

9. Ibid., p. 143.

10. "Proceso del pensamiento venezolano," in *Obras selectas,* p. 193.

11. Ibid.

12. "La finalidad poco americana de una literatura," p. 148.

13. "Los sermones de Díaz-Rodríguez," in *Buscando el camino,* p. 78.

14. "La finalidad poco americana de una literatura," p. 147.

15. Ibid., p. 34.

16. "Días de marcha," in *Obras selectas,* p. 1383.

17. "Mozas campesinas," in *Buscando el camino,* p. 34.

18. "Los dos abuelos," in *Buscando el camino,* p. 34.

Chapter Four

1. Mariano Picón Salas, *Problemas y metódos de la historia del arte* (Santiago, 1934), p. 25.

2. G. W. F. Hegel, *Selections,* ed. J. Lowenstein (New York, 1929), p. xiii.

3. "Tentación de la literatura," in *Obras selectas,* p. 1356.

4. J. M. Siso Martínez, *Mariano Picón Salas* (Mexico City, 1970), p. 35.

5. Hegel, *Selections,* p. 438.

6. "Antíthesis y tesis de nuestra historia," in *Obras selectas,* p. 207.

7. "Proceso del pensamiento venezolano," in *Obras selectas,* p. 176.

8. *Mundo imaginario,* p. 16.

9. *Odisea de tierra firme,* p. 47.

10. Ibid., p. 49.

11. *Obras selectas,* p. 1364.

12. "Adolescencia," p. 1346.

13. *Mundo imaginario,* p. 49.

14. Ibid., p. 50.

15. "El año 1920," in *Obras selectas,* p. 1365.

Chapter Five

1. "El año 1920," p. 1367.
2. Raymond E. Crist and Edward P. Leahy, *Venezuela: Search for a Middle Ground* (New York, 1969), p. 64; Edwin Lieuwen, *Venezuela* (London, 1961), pp. 1–63.
3. See Hubert Herring, *Latin America* (New York, 1955), p. 468: ". . . Gomez's rule was harsh. A powerful army, numerous police, and ubiquitous spies scrutinized the acts and words of every citizen. Jails and dungeons were crowded with thousands of political prisoners, committed without trial and held without appeal."
4. Laureano Vallenilla Lanz, *Cesarismo democrático* (Caracas, 1929), pp. 175–212.
5. "Estación de Caracas," in *Obras selectas*, 1368; this essay will hereafter be cited in the text as *E*.
6. A view of the early intellectual formation of Picón Salas is offered by the author in *Viaje al amanecer* in the essay entitled "Política y religión en el escritorio de abuelo."
7. The battle at Ayacucho in 1824 was a final victory by the revolutionary forces led by General Antonio Sucre. It secured Peruvian independence and the triumph of the revolution against the Spaniards.
8. "Días de Marcha," in *Obras selectas*, p. 1378; this essay will hereafter be cited in the text as *D*.
9. "Para un retrato de Alberto Adriani," in *Obras selectas*, pp. 349–69.
10. Beginning with José María Heredia, Spanish American literature is replete with the theme of exile and the nostalgia for homeland produced by an existence in exile.
11. "En la *Fértil Provincia* señalada," in *Obras selectas*, p. 1340; this essay will hereafter be cited in the text as *F*.
12. "Intuición de Chile," in *Intuición de Chile* (Santiago, 1935), p. 17. The reference to the Merovingian kings relates to their position as "do-nothing" rulers leaving the governing of the land to the feudal lords. The concept that Picón Salas was trying to convey was that in Chile the leaders, due to the code of *el disimulo*, were forced to project an image of do-nothingness.
13. Rosas, Guzmán Blanco, and García Moreno were all nineteenth-century dictators of their respective countries—Argentina, Venezuela, and Ecuador.
14. See *Odisea de tierra firme* and *Los días de Cipriano Castro* for an analysis and description of tropicalism.
15. Fagg, *Latin America, a General History*, pp. 675–78.
16. The only reference to the essay written by Picón Salas is by the

author himself in "Días de marcha." I have been unable to locate it in any of my research.

17. The correspondence between Adriani and Picón Salas has not been discovered. A possibility does exist that these letters, as well as others, are in the possession of Picón's daughter. I have not had access to any of this material.

18. "Amor, en fin que todo diga y cante," in *Obras selectas*, p. 1406; this essay will hereafter be cited in the text as *A*.

19. "Vicisitud de la política," in *Obras selectas*, p. 1441; this essay will hereafter be cited in the text as *V*.

20. "De la libertad intelectual," *El Nacional* (Caracas), January 19, 1950.

21. Hubert Herring, *Latin America* (New York, 1955) p. 664.

22. "Para un retrato de Alberto Adriani," in *Obras selectas*, p. 360; this essay will hereafter be cited in the text as *R*.

23. J. M. Siso Martínez, *Mariano Picón Salas*, p. 28. The secondary source for this letter was used since the original was unavailable to me.

24. "Regreso y promisión," in *Obras selectas*, p. 1431; this essay will hereafter be cited in the text as *Re*.

25. "La palabra revolución," in *Obras selectas*, p. 1415; this essay will hereafter be cited in the text as *L*.

26. Siso Martínez, *Mariano Picón Salas*, p. 15.

27. Guillermo Morón, *A History of Venezuela*, ed. and trans. John Street (London, 1964), pp. 205–6.

28. *Miranda* (Buenos Aires, 1946), p. 10. In this biography of Francisco de Miranda's life, the author refers to the precursor of Venezuelan Independence as a synthesis of Venezuelan manhood ("hombre síntesis").

29. *Mundo imaginario*, p. 22.

30. "Añorantes moradas," in *Obras selectas*, p. 1445; this essay will hereafter be cited in the text as *M*.

31. *Registro de huéspedes*, p. 118.

Chapter Six

1. "Meditación francesa," in *Obras selectas*, p. 1096.
2. "Meditación alemana," in *Obras selectas*, p. 1109.
3. "Italia," in *Obras selectas*, p. 1147.
4. "Eternos símbolos de españa," in *Obras selectas*, p. 1156.
5. "Reino de bohemia, reino de Dios," in *Obras selectas*, p. 1131.
6. "Mayo 1940," in *Obras selectas*, p. 1203.
7. *Comprensión de Venezuela* (Caracas, 1949), p. 55.
8. "La buena vecindad," in *Obras selectas*, p. 1211.
9. "Profecía de la palabra," in *Obras selectas*, p. 1258.
10. *Comprensión de Venezuela*, p. 54

Chapter Seven

1. *Viaje al amanecer* (Mexico City, 1943), p. 54.
2. Ibid., p. 46.
3. Ibid., p. 47.
4. Ibid.
5. *1941: Cinco discursos sobre pasado y presente de la nación venezolana* (Caracas, 1940), p. 9.
6. *Viaje al amanecer*, p. 21.
7. "Pequeño tratado de la tradición," in *Obras selectas*, pp. 950–65.
8. *Viaje al amanecer*, p. 191.
9. The myth of Maricastaña represents Spanish antiquity. In Latin America, where the traditions of peninsular culture remained fairly intact throughout history, the notion of Maricastaña lived, and still does, in the expression *en los tiempos de Maricastaña* ("in the times of Maricastaña"). The expression alludes to an indefinite time in the past, a period of time that cannot be regained. Maricastaña personifies an eternal symbol of tradition. Removed from the particular events of history, Maricastaña presents the past as legend and mystery.
10. *Viaje al amanecer*, p. 17.
11. Ibid., p. 15.
12. Ibid., p. 16.
13. Ibid., p. 23.
14. Ibid.
15. Ibid., p. 22.
16. Ibid., p. 23.
17. Ibid., p. 25.
18. "Los anticristos," in *Obras selectas*, p. 1271.

Chapter Eight

1. Martin S. Stabb, *América Latina en busca de una identidad*, trans. Mario Giacchino (Caracas, 1969), p. 327.
2. *Comprensión de Venezuela*, p. 157.
3. Ibid., p. 158.
4. "Dirección: punto omega," in *Los malos salvajes*, p. 110.
5. "Misterio americano," in *Obras selectas*, p. 570.

Selected Bibliography

PRIMARY SOURCES

1. Books and Editions

Las nuevas corrientes del arte. Dissertation, Universidad de los Andes de Mérida, October 28, 1917. Mérida, Venezuela: El Tapiz, 1917. This essay is a reprint of Picón Salas' first public appearance as a lecturer.

En las puertas de un mundo nuevo (Ensayo de crítica social). Mérida, Venezuela: Universitatis Andinensis, 1918.

Buscando el camino. Caracas: Editorial Cultural Venezolana, 1920. The author's first major collection of essays.

Mundo imaginario. Los recuerdos impresionistas. La vida de un hombre. Historia de un amigo. Tema de amor. Santiago de Chile: Editorial Nascimento, 1927.

Hispano-américa, posición crítica. Ediciones de Índice, Arte y Literatura, 3. Santiago de Chile: Imprenta Universitaria, 1931. I discovered a copy of this work in the *Casa Hispánica* of Columbia University. It is not to be found in the National Library in Caracas. Another interesting note is that this copy had a dedication inscribed to Waldo Frank.

Odisea de tierra firme. Santiago de Chile: Zig-Zag, 1931; 2d ed., 1940

Problemas y métodos de la historia del arte: Dos conferencias didácticas. Santiago de Chile: Editorial Nascimento, 1934.

Registro de huéspedes. Santiago de Chile: Editorial Nascimento, 1934. In this work Picón Salas announced the preparation of a novel entitled "Travesía de un hombre sin plata," as well as a collection of essays, "Viaje al pasado." Neither of these two works have been published. It is possible that the notes for the novel are in the possession of Picón Salas' daughter Delia Isabel, and that "Viaje al pasado" was the initial title for *Intuición de Chile y otros ensayos en busca de una conciencia histórica.*

Intuición de Chile y otros ensayos en busca de una conciencia histórica. Santiago de Chile: Ercilla, 1935

Preguntas a Europa. Viajes y ensayos. Santiago de Chile: Zig-Zag, 1937. A note in the *Revista Hispánica Moderna,* 5, no. 1 (January,

1939), 84, indicated that this book was translated by the Czech writer Rud Slaby. Slaby, also, lectured on March 18, 1938, on the significance of Picón Salas' cultural observations and the latter's ability to capture in his essays the essence of the national spirit of Czechoslovakia.

Europa-América. Preguntas a la esfinge de la cultura. México: Ediciones Cuadernos Americanos, 1947.

1941: Cinco discursos sobre el pasado y presente de la nación venezolana. Caracas: Editorial La Torre, 1940.

Un viaje y seis retratos. Caracas: Cuadernos Literarios de la Asociación de Escritores Venezolanos, Editorial Elite, 1940.

Formación y proceso de la literatura venezolana. Caracas: Editorial Cecilio Acosta, 1940; 2d ed., 1945; 3d ed., 1948; 4th ed., 1952.

Estudios de literatura venezolana. Caracas-Madrid: Ediciones Edime, 1961. This edition is a complete revision of *Literatura venezolana*. The reason given, by Picón Salas, for this revision was that *Literatura venezolana* had been pirated by other publishers.

Viaje al amanecer. Prólogo de Ermilo Abreu Gómez. Mexico City: Ediciones Mensaje, 1943. Other editions: Buenos Aires: Editorial Losada, 1948; Caracas: Ediciones Nueva Cádiz, 1956; [Lima]: Ediciones Nuevo Mundo, 1962; *Voyage au point du jour.* Translated by Jean and André Catrysse, preface by René L. F. Durand. Paris: Nouvelles Editions Latines, n.d. I have only seen mention of this translation in a footnote. The date of publication is unavailable.

De la conquista a la independencia: Tres siglos de historia cultural hispanoamericana. Mexico City: Fondo de Cultura Económica, 1944; 2d ed. rev., 1950; 3d ed., 1958.

A Cultural History of Spanish America: From Conquest to Independence. Translated and with a forward by Irving Leonard. Berkeley: University of California Press, 1962.

Miranda. Buenos Aires: Editorial Losada, 1946; 2d ed., 1955.

Comprensión de Venezuela. Caracas: Ministerio de Educación Nacional, 1949; rev. ed., 1955.

Pedro Claver, el santo de los esclavos. Mexico City: Fondo de Cultura Económico, 1950; 2d ed., 1954; 3d ed., 1959.

Dependencia e independencia en la historia hispanoamericana. Caracas: Librería "Cruz del Sur," 1952.

Gusto de México. México: Porrúa y Obregón, 1952; 2d ed., 1952.

Los días de Cipriano Castro. Caracas: Garrido, 1953; 2d ed., 1955.

Simón Rodríguez (1771–1854). Caracas: Ediciones de la Fundación Mendoza, 1953.

Suramérica: período colonial. Instituto Panamericano de Geografía e historia. Vol. 58, pt. 2. Mexico City: Editorial Fournier, 1953. This book is not a study but a syllabus of instruction.

Los tratos de la noche. Barquisimeto, Venezuela: Editorial Nueva
   Segovia, 1955.
Crisis, cambios y tradición. La crisis y el aire de nuestra cultura. Cara-
   cas: Ediciones Edime, 1955.
Las nieves de antaño: Pequeña añoranza de Mérida. Maracaibo:
   Ediciones de la Universidad de Zulia, 1958.
Despedida do Brasil. Translated by Arino Peres. Rio de Janeiro: As-
   sociaçao Brasileira do Congresso pela Liberdade da Cultura, 1959.
Regreso de tres mundos. Un hombre en su generación. Mexico City:
   Fondo de Cultura Económico, 1959.
Au carrefour de trois mondes. Translated by M. O. Fortier and M.
   Serrat. Paris: Casterman, 1964.
Los malos salvajes. Civilización y política contemporáneas. Buenos
   Aires: Editorial Sudamericano, 1962.
The Ignoble Savages. Translated by Hubert Weinstock. New York:
   Knopf, 1965.
Hora y deshora; temas humanísticos, nombres y figuras, viajes y lugares.
   Caracas: Editorial Arte, 1963.
2.   Essays in *El Nacional*
"Post-guerra e interamericanismo," March 5, 1944.
"Sobre una posible integración hispano-americana," July 16, 1944.
"En el P.E.N. Club de México," July 23, 1944.
"La tierra maternal de Venezuela," August 20, 1944.
"Barroco literario de Índias," December 3, 1944.
"Juan Antonio Pérez Bonalde," January 27, 1946.
"Perón y el peronismo," February 7, 1946.
"Pólvora en Guanajuato," March 24, 1946.
"Historia de un anti-héroe," August 15, 1946.
"Cajas de estrépitos," August 25, 1946.
"Miranda," October 20, 1946.
"Cuento de cuentos," November 3, 1946.
"Una isla azotada," January 21, 1947.
"Palabras con Don Pedro Emilio," April 27, 1947.
"Rumbo de Venezuela," May 15, 1947.
"Politización," May 20, 1947.
"Invocación del estadista," May 25, 1947.
"De la historia en Venezuela," December 25, 1947.
"Iniciación centro-americano," March 5, 1949.
"Dulzura y tremor en Guatemala," March 11, 1949.
"Juego y cortesía," March 18, 1949.
"Jasón buscando divisas," March 25, 1949.
"Zona de ángeles," March 27, 1949.
"Parcas y Euménides de México," April 16, 1949.
"Ningún lugar para ocultarse," April 22, 1949.
"Piedras y Salas," April 29, 1949.

"El ejemplo de Varona," May 6, 1949.

"Coloquio cubano," May 13, 1949.

"Técnica y volcanes," May 19, 1949.

"A medio km. de la gran pirámide," May 27, 1949.

"Shakespeare y el cine," June 3, 1949.

"Los que viven por sus manos," June 10, 1949.

"Del optimismo a la previsión económica," June 17, 1949.

"Un eclesiastés petrolero," June 24, 1949.

"Pequeña historia de un poeta frustrado," July 8, 1949.

"Momias," July 22, 1949.

"Signo del calor. Fragmento de un estudio sobre Venezuela," August 3, 1948.

"Don Vasco," August 5, 1949.

"Turistas y evadidos," August 19, 1949.

"Tercer premio de nuestro concurso de cuentos," August 21, 1949.

"Cristo de Campo," August 26, 1949.

"Inventos mexicanos," August 28, 1949.

"Addenda a los mandamientos," August 31, 1949.

"Diego el gigante fiel," September 9, 1949.

"Tiempo de Goethe," September 11, 1949.

"Trabajos sobre Bello," September 16, 1949.

"Una ciudad en la estepa," September 30, 1949.

"Ritualismo y economía," October 8, 1949.

"Hombres y dioses del maíz," October 14, 1949.

"Las repúblicas desunidas," October 21, 1949.

"A veinte años de Doña Barbara," October 31, 1949.

"Un libro que nos concierne," November 18, 1949.

"Viaje a los orígenes, el impacto inicial," November 20, 1949.

"Mítica americana y libros de caballería," November 25, 1949.

"El reino de este mundo," November 27, 1949.

"Historia reformada," December, 1949.

"Colombia," December 9, 1949.

"De la libertad intelectual," December 16, 1949.

"Crisis y miseria de los libros," December 26, 1949.

"Provincias," January 6, 1950.

"Viviendas para muchos," January 13, 1950.

"Aventuras de las ideas en América," January 20, 1950.

"Diferencias americanas," February 3, 1950.

"Existencialismo," February 10, 1950.

"Cultura y sosiego," February 17, 1950.

"Cifras venezolanas," February 24, 1950.

"Marte Express," March 24, 1950.

"Los enciclopedistas," March 17, 1950.

"Miranda," March 28, 1950.

"Viaje por nuestra historia," March 31, 1950.

"Misterios, cada día," April 9, 1950.
"Economía estratégica y economía de paz," April 15, 1950.
"Ixtapalapa," April 21, 1950.
"Lola y sus manos," May 2, 1950.
"Historia y arte," May 5, 1950.
"Un Pentateuco," June 9, 1950.
"Indigenismo mexicano," June 10, 1950.
"La América Hispana en Miranda," June 11, 1950.
"Cocina y nacionalidad," June 16, 1950.
"Una crónica del estío," August 10, 1950.
"Palomas en Manhattan," September 17, 1950.
"Año nuevo judío," September 24, 1950.
"Los españoles y nosotros," November 12, 1950.
"Bernard Shaw en tiempo pasado," November 19, 1950.
"Premios Nobel," December 4, 1950.
"Requiem de algunos amigos," December 11, 1950.
"Literatura enconmendada," December 18, 1950.
"Barbarismos y venezolanismos," December 26, 1950.
"Caracas, allí está," January 1, 1951.
"Sarmiento y Monsier Guizot," January 4, 1951.
"Navidad y otras vísperas," January 16, 1951.
"San José en la O.E.A.," January 23, 1951.
"Estudiantes hispano-americanos," February 14, 1951.
"Proceso de una película," February 27, 1951.
"Televisión," March 13, 1951.
"El complejo de Marco Polo," April 4, 1951.
"Argentina," June 3, 1952.
"El Rey de las basuras," August 28, 1951.
"Caracas y Tulsa, Oklahoma," September 2, 1951.
"Hearst, El emperador amarillo," September 5, 1951.
"Lógica en la ciudad," September 19, 1951.
"Palabras de un escritor español," September 23, 1951.
"El fenómeno telúrico," September 30, 1951.
"Almanaques," October 14, 1951.
"Ser y devenir en la historia," October 28, 1951.
"Campo y comida," November 2, 1951.
"Las formas y las visiones," November 9, 1951.
"Las ideas en las entrañas," November 14, 1951.
"Las formas y las visiones, II," November 16, 1951.
"Cartas de Teresa de la Parra," November 23, 1951.
"La semana de Bello, pequeño escolio bellista," November 30, 1951.
"Terceto de voces sobre la crítica literaria," December 13, 1951.
"Un libro de historia," December 14, 1951.
"Cuando la navidad deja de ser venezolana," December 21, 1951.
"Modus Moriendi," December 28, 1951.

"Oro," January 4, 1952.
"Estrellas y mariposas," March 24, 1952.
"Salón y museo," March 31, 1952.
"Hambre y conocimiento," April 7, 1952.
"La reina humanista," April 14, 1952.
"Primera nota sobre Leonardo: La época," April 22, 1952.
"Segunda nota sobre Leonardo: problemas," April 29, 1952.
"Tradición y voluntad histórica," May 6, 1952.
"Entre lo dicho y lo omitido," May 12, 1952.
"Civilización palabra frágil," May 13, 1952.
"Ascensos y descensos en la historia nacional," May 20, 1952.
"Aventura en la historia," May 27, 1952.
"La república mercantil," June 10, 1952.
"Cardones y hombres," July 1, 1952.
"Símbolos del caracol," July 15, 1952.
"Exámenes," July 22, 1952.
"El wikingo de Antioquía," August 5, 1952.
"Aproximación al Orinoco," August 12, 1952.
"Formas de lo cursi," August 19, 1952.
"Dentro y fuera," August 26, 1952.
"Andar a pie," September 2, 1952.
"Crisis social en Colombia," September 16, 1952.
"Nuestra alma en el teatro," September 23, 1952.
"Actualidad de un libro viejo," September 30, 1952.
"Una tradición educativa," October 7, 1952.
"Sanz, justicia mayor," October 13, 1952.
"Lo bueno, sí breve," October 21, 1952.
"Breve meditación del *Quo Vadis*," October 28, 1952.
"La estatua del viejo Guzmán," November 18, 1952.
"Palabras y sociedad," November 25, 1952.
"Un gran testimonio mexicano," December 1, 1952.
"Curazao: primera imagen," December 23, 1952.
"Heterodoxia en Curazao," December 30, 1952.
"Simadan," January 6, 1953.
"Signos y presencias," January 15, 1953.
"Caracas y la Habana," January 18, 1953.
"Despedida de Cuba," February 12, 1953.
"Para una historia de América," February 18, 1953.
"Signos y presencia. Pensamiento venezolano," March 12, 1953.
"Signos y presencias. Poetas venezolanos en francés," March 26, 1953.
"Litografía del septenio," May 14, 1953.
"Coloquio en Valera," July 13, 1953.
"Nota sobre Camilo José Cela," July 30, 1953.
"Vida y trabajo en los Andes," August 3, 1953.
"Las Américas en su historia," August 12, 1953.

"Los alegres avisos," August 19, 1953.
"Boussingault, amable memorialista," August 26, 1953.
"Nuestro aire cultural," October 8, 1953.
"Nuestro aire cultural. Nota segunda: El aire de la literatura," October, 15, 1953.
"Memorias de Blanco Fombona," October 16, 1953.
"Saludo a Américo Castro," January 22, 1954.
"Pequeña confesión a la sordina," January 29, 1954.
"La taza de café," February 14, 1954.
"Escollos de Matías Salazar," February 17, 1954.
"Ceniza de Simón Rodriguez," February 24, 1954.
"Cultura de Mérida," March 4, 1954.
"Setecientos años de Marco Polo," March 18, 1954.
"Y va de ensayo," May 26, 1954.
"Jornadas de tierra firme," June 2, 1954.
"Aproximación a la crisis," June 26, 1954.
"Aproximación a la crisis," July 3, 1954.
"Centenario del Dr. Vargas," July 13, 1954.
"Margen a Alí Lameda," July 17, 1954.
"Prólogo a Mallea," July 25, 1954.
"Arte y libertad creadora," August 14, 1954.
"Cocina romántica," August 21, 1954.
"Los chismes del enviado," August 28, 1954.
"La pintura de Reverón," September 30, 1954.
"El cambio de los tiempos," October 21, 1954.
"Fermín Toro, hombre recordable," February 3, 1955.
"En defensa de la pintura venezolana," February 5, 1955.
"Ciencia y Humanidades," February 23, 1955.
"En la Universidad de los Andes," March 31, 1955.
"Pequeño tratado de la tradición," June 3–5, 1955.
"Varón humanismo," June 8, 1955.
"La cultura francesa y nosostros," June 20, 1955.
"López Méndez y el positivismo venezolano," June 28, 1955.
"Ejemplos del modernismo venezolano," July 14, 1955.
"La lengua impura," July 18, 1955.
"Dos libros sobre nuestros orígenes," July 28, 1955.
"Fin de semana," November 17, 1955.
"Pocaterra," December 8, 1955.
"Humanistas," January 21, 1956.
"Los escritores y las circunstancias venezolanas," February 8, 1956.
"Otra Mérida," March 27, 1956.
"Retrato de un país," April 7, 1956.
"El cordial visitante," April 11, 1956.
"Primera plática de inmigrantes," April 18, 1956.
"Testimonio de inmigrantes," May 9, 1956.

"Profesiones," May 23, 1956.
"Sarmiento otra vez," May 30, 1956.
"Tema de un debate," June 6, 1956.
"Calor de Coro," June 12, 1956.
"Palabras de amistad," June 19, 1956.
"El explorador de las palabras," June 26, 1956.
"Diez años de la facultad de Humanidades," November 7, 1956.
"Jubileo de los libros," November 21, 1956.
"Estampillas de Francia," December 5, 1956.
"Vicisitudes en el arte de historiar," December 31, 1956.
"Testimonio de Gabriela," January 11, 1957.
"Una novela de la inseguridad," January 25, 1957.
"El Dr. Lisandro Alvarado," January 31, 1957.
"El Dr. Lisandro Alvarado," February 1, 1957.
"Palabras en la victoria," February 14, 1957.
"Teatro y Poesía," May 8, 1957.
"Respuesta final a Teo Calcaño," May 14, 1957.
"Ciudades de Cumpleaños," October 8, 1957.
"Testimonio de Mérida. Monseñor Dr. Rafael Lazo de la Vega,"
    October 15, 1957.
"El último Inca," October 19, 1957.
"Viejos y nuevos mundos," November 5, 1957.
"Historias provinciales," November 10, 1957.
"Grandes anales de 15 días," January 25, 1958.
"Los prudentes Ulises y el buen gobierno," February 7, 1958.
"Los independientes," February 14, 1958.
"Unidad de hombres, no de ángeles," February 25, 1958.
"Palabras a Rómulo Gallegos," March 12, 1958.
"Mujiquita, treinta años después," March 14, 1958.
"Golpismo y demagogia," March 21, 1958.
"Pequeñas experiencias democráticas," May 3, 1958.
"Universidades," May 6, 1958.
"Recuerdo de Mario," June 23, 1958.
"Humanismo hace dos mil años," July 24, 1958.
"Vicisitud de la política," August 7, 1958.
"Velada en Río," August 7, 1958.
"Mensaje a los merideños en el IV centenario de la ciudad," September
    25, 1958.
"Bolívar en el Brasil," October 31, 1958.
"Cumpleaños," January 31, 1959.
"Bolívar entre los libros," April 24, 1959.
"La cobardía intelectual," August 12, 1959.
"La ley es la libertad," August 19, 1959.
"Trato a la tierra," September 5, 1959.
"Marca de Austria," October 5, 1959.

"Historia de un pecado mortal," October 9, 1959.
"Estudiantes," October 26, 1959.
"Teatro y disparate," November 4, 1959.
"Las diásporas de España o la España de la libertad," November 27, 1959.
"Sesiones de la UNESCO," December 17, 1959.
"Noosfera parisiense," December 26, 1959.
"Letra de Alfonso Reyes," January 16, 1960.
"Más allá del alboroto," January 25, 1960.
"Europeos y americanos," February 1, 1960.
"Carta a Juan Liscano," February 4, 1960.
"México en Octavio Paz," February 11, 1960.
"Bolivar entre muchos testigos," February 14, 1960.
"Entre la esperanza y la frustración," April 5, 1960.
"Entre el tumulto y las cadenas," July 2, 1960.
"Sociología de lo apocalíptico," July 23, 1960.
"Y la ciudad está allí," July 24, 1960.
"Culpa y responsabilidad," July 24, 1960.
"El poeta abuelo," September 4, 1960.
"La UNESCO y la utopía humana," November 28, 1960.
"Paseo suizo," January 24, 1961.
"Suiza: segunda nota," January 25, 1961.
"Follaje diabólico," April 3, 1961.
"La ruta en la ceniza," April 4, 1961.
"Imagen del infierno," April 5, 1961.
"Meditación junto al pernod," April 6, 1961.
"Desengaño y novelería," May 16, 1961.
"El tema novelero," May 17, 1961.
"Lo novelero en Madame Bovary," May 18, 1961.
"Visita a San Antonio," September 10, 1961.
"Visita a los malos salvajes," September 30, 1961.
"La iglesia sin ritos," October 1, 1961.
"Nausea y compañía," October 2, 1961.
"Un hombre con un saco de huesos," October 29, 1961.
"Hombre y biología," October 30, 1961.
"Angustia e historia," October 31, 1961.
"Punto Omega," November 1, 1961.
"Mitos y formas del subdesarrollo," February 8, 1962.
"Lo continente americano," February 9, 1962.
"Amistad con Europa," February 10, 1962.
"Terrorismo," March 16, 1962.
"El hombre del proyecto mayor," April 1, 1962.
"Entre dioses y hombres," April 26, 1962.
"Entre prosistas venezolanos," January 24, 1963.
"La gran esperanza," July 12, 1963.

"Las tumbas intranquilas," July 19, 1963.
"El origen," August 3, 1963.
"Bachilleres, 63," August 5, 1963.
"La democracia," December 8, 1963.
"Autonomía y sacralización," May 26, 1964.
"Caracas, la malquerida," June 5, 1964.
"La linea China," June 12, 1964.
"En el Lepanto Universitario," June 19, 1964.
"Poetas," June 26, 1964.
"Fotografías," July 3, 1964.
"Gallegos en Doña Barbara (al cumplir ochenta años)," August 3, 1964.
"Perfil de Caracas (hace veinte años)," January 3, 1965.
"Luto en la familia, Ateneo," January 20, 1965.
"Papel literario," February 7, 1965.
"Entre prosistas venezolanos, papel literario," August 22, 1965.

3. Anthologies
Obras selectas. Caracas: Ediciones Edime, 1953; 2d ed., 1962.
Ensayos escogidos. Preface by Ricardo Latcham. Selected by Juan
   Loveluck. Santiago de Chile: Editora Zig-Zag, 1958.

4. Books Edited with Other Authors
PICÓN SALAS, MARIANO, and FELIÚ CRUZ, GUILLERMO. *Imágenes de
   Chile.* Santiago: Editorial Nascimento, 1933. This book is a col-
   lection of essays and pictures dealing with the life and times in
   Chile in the eighteenth and nineteenth century.

SECONDARY SOURCES

AZZARIO, ESTHER. "Mariano Picón Salas, poeta." *Asomante,* 1, no. 26,
   51–57. The only discussion about several published poems by
   the author.
BACUI, STEFAN. "Mariano Picón Salas, desconocido." *La Torre,* 69
   (1970), 69–91. A very interesting series of anecdotes about Picón
   Salas in Brazil. Demonstrates the essayist's spiritual commitment
   to all of Latin American culture.
BELTRÁN GUERRERO, LUIS. "El gran Mariano." *Candideces,* 4th ser.
   (1972), 191–99. A view of Picón Salas as a poet of ideas. The
   author as a man for all seasons who did not allow himself to become consumed by political ambition.
————. "Rufino y Mariano." *Candideces,* 4th ser. (1972), 68–71.
   Identifies the mutual respect that existed between Rufino Blanco
   Fombona and Mariano Picón Salas in spite of the fact that both
   writers differed widely in their approach to life.

BENTE, THOMAS O. "Man and Dircumstance: A Study of Mariano Picón Salas' Work." Ph.D. dissertation, University of California at Los Angeles, 1968. General analysis of the essayist's work beginning in 1933. The author is seen as a man of his time.

BETANCOURT, RÓMULO. "Dos libros de Picón Salas." Repertorio Americano (San José, Costa Rica), 22 (June 20, 1931), 364–69. A political discussion of Odisea de Tierra Firme and Hispanoamérica, posición crítica. Agrees with Picón Salas that Venezuelan history, beginning with the Wars of Federation, can be viewed as a bilateral contract between cuadillismo and the forces of imperialism.

CANO, JOSE LUIS, "Mariano Picón Salas." Cuadernos americanos, 182 (1965), 321–24. A view of the author as a man totally dedicated to his work. Author and the man are one.

CARMONA NENCLARES, F. "Mariano Picón Salas: Formación y proceso." Letras, 5 (1942), 117–21. Argues, as have several critics, that Picón Salas' Formación y proceso de la literatura venezolana offered, when published, one of the best interpretations of the interaction between Venezuelan literature and society.

Discursos leídos en el acto de la recepción pública del académico de número Don Mariano Picón Salas. Colección de Augusto Mijares. Caracas: Academia Nacional de la Historia, 1947. Collection of speeches honoring Picón Salas and his contributions to Venezuelan culture at the time when the essayist accepted nomination to the Venezuelan Academy of History.

GRASES, PEDRO. "Acerca de Mariano Picón Salas." Investigaciones. Vol. 2. Caracas: Ministerio de Educación. Departamento de Puclicaciones, 1968. Pp. 159–95. Broadly discusses the main thrust of the author's thought. Article also appeared as "Las ideas fundamentales de Mariano Picón Salas," in Mapocho, 5, no. 1 (1966), 217–32, and as "Mariano Picón Salas o la Inquietud Hispanoamericana," published by Editorial Arte in 1966.

————. "Un humanista de América." Revista Américas, 18, no. 6 June, 1965), 6–10. Draws parallels between the work of Picón Salas and that of Alfonso Reyes.

LEIGH, HERNAN and DE LA PRESA, RAFAEL. "Homenaje a la memoria del escritor venezolano Mariano Picón Salas, fallecido recientemente. Nota de condolencia," La Nación (Santiago de Chile), January 8, 1965, p. 11. Addresses to the Chilean Congress on the occasion of Picón Salas' untimely death. Recognition of the essayist's contributions to Chile.

LOVELUCK, JUAN. "Mariano Picón Salas." Revista Iberoamericana, 31, no. 60 (1965), 263–76. A general overview of the essential works of the essayist.

MEAD, ROBERT. "Mariano Picón Salas y otros voces de protesta en el moderno ensayo hispanoamericano." Cuadernos Americanos,

202 (1975), 97–108. Discusses Picón Salas optimism about life and protest against modern society along with the ideas of Sebastián Salazar Bondy, Carlos Fuentes, Octavio Paz, and Mario Vargas Llosa.

PINEDA, RAFAEL, ed. *Para Mariano Picón Salas.* Caracas: Instituto Nacional de Cultura y Bellas Artes, 1966. Published as a festschriften, this book is a collection of articles by Venezuelan and other Latin American intellectuals written at the time of Picón Salas' death.

PLA Y BELTRÁN. "Un escritor de América." *Revista Nacional de Cultura,* 19, no. 119 (1956), 65–73. Concludes that Picón Salas is one of the great humanists of the twentieth century.

Política (Caracas), 4, no. 39 (April–May, 1965), entire issue. This edition published as a festschriften. Most articles were first presented as papers on the French radio and television station Europa 65, in March, 1965. Articles by Ermilo Abreu Gómez, Germán Arciniegas, Benjamín Carrión, Humberto Díaz-Casanueva, Gastón Figueira, Gilberto Freire, Elena Martínez Chacón, Juan Oropesa, Lucila Palacios, Luis Pastori, Luis B. Prieto F., Arturo Uslar Pietri, and Luis Alberto Sánchez.

ROSENBLAT, ANGEL. "Mariano Picón Salas: El estilo y el hombre." *Thesaurus* (Boletín del Instituto Caro y Cuervo), 20, no. 2 (1965), 201–2. Establishes the relationship between Picón Salas, the writer, and Picón Salas, the man.

_____ "Mariano Picón Salas." *La primera visión de América y otros estudios.* Caracas: Departamento de Publicaciones del Ministerio de Educación, 1969. Pp. 223–48. Identifies the universal perspective in Picón Salas' thought and how the essayist became a symbol for an entire generation of Latin American students and intellectuals.

SÁNCHEZ CARRILLO, ANTONIO. "El mensaje de Mariano Picón Salas." *Cuadernos Americanos,* 82 (1955), 143–48. Discusses Picón Salas important message to modern technological society: the need to incorporate the humanistic traditions of antiquity into contemporary life.

SILVA CASTRO, RAUL. "Mariano Picón Salas." *El Mercurio* (Santiago de Chile), January, 1965. Of special interest because it provides information not widely publicized about the literary group *Indice* which Picón Salas helped organize during the thirties in Chile.

SISO MARTÍNEZ, J. M. *Mariano Picón Salas (Ensayo inacabade).* Caracas: Editorial Yocoima, 1970. The first book length study on Picón Salas. Offers a broad overview of the essayist' ideas and their relationship to the political reality in Venezuela at the time. Fairly informative.

USLAR PIETRI, ARTURO. "El regreso de los mundos de Mariano Picón Salas." In *En busca del nuevo mundo.* Mexico City: Fondo de

Cultura Económica, 1969. Pp. 161–67. Discusses Picón Salas as a
man of conscience.

Index

Acosta, Cecilio, 25
Adriani, Alberto, 78, 95
Alessandri, Arturo, 82, 88
Años de literatura venezolana, 50 (Medina), 32
Antichrist, The, 101

Barrios, Eduardo, 83, 92
Bello, Andrés, 30
Beltrán Guerrero, Luis, 26
Bergson, Henri, 28
Betancourt, Rómulo, 86
Biblioteca de escritores venezolanos (Rojas), 32
Blanco, Andrés Eloy, 27
Bolívar Simón, 17–18, 20, 26, 43, 52,58–60, 82, 87, 128
Boutroux, Emile, 28
Byron, 47

Caballero, Nieto, 90
Calvin, 85
Cantos de peregrino (Mármol), 24
Castro, Cipriano, 25, 38, 74, 96
caudillo, 17, 41, 96
caudillismo, 18–19, 31, 64, 74–75, 80, 127; *See also* Wise, George S.
Cesarismo democráctico (Vallenilla Lanz), 74
Cervantes, 36
Chardin, Teilhard de, 65
Comenius, Jan Amos, 107
Continente enfermo, El (Arguedas), 28
Cortés, Hernán, 23
criollo, 43, 44, 64
Croce, Benedetto, 115
cultura (culture), meaning of, 112, 115
cultural authenticity, 40; *See also* Venezolanidad and Picón Salas

de la Nuez, Antonio, 35
de la Parra, Teresa, 30

de las Casa, Bartolomé, 70
del Solar, Hernán, 93
devenir (becoming), meaning of, 62–64; *See also* Picón Salas
Díaz del Castillo, Bernal, 23
Díaz, Porfirio, 19
Díaz Rodríguez, Manuel, 47
Disgregación e integración (Vallenilla Lanz), 18
Doña Bárbara (Gallegos), 66
Donoso, Armando, 92
Don Quixote, 73, 76, 108; *See also* Picón Salas
Dostoevski, 92

Estilo de Alfonso Reyes, El (Robb), 34
Ernst, Adolfo, 25
errancia (peregrination), 22, 52–56, 67, 72–73, 91, 93, 95, 118, 121; as a quest, 44; errancia venezolana (Venezuelan peregrination), 24; meaning of, 42–44; *See also* Picón Salas
essay, 34–35; ensayismo, 35; problems in, 37–38; *See also* de la Nuez, Martínez, Picón Salas, Ripoll, and Zum Felde

Facundo (Sarmiento), 21, 66
Falcón, Juan Crisóstomo, 19
fantasía bárbara, meaning of, 119
Fortoul, José Gil, 58
Freud, 84
Fuenzalida, Hector, 93

Gallegos, Rómulo, 95
García Monge, Joaquín, 90
García Moreno, Gabriel, 19
Gaspar Rodríguez, José, 18
Generation of 1918, 27–28, 48
Generation of 1928, 28–29

Gómez, Juan Vicente, 19, 25, 38, 74–78,
    82–85, 88–90, 94, 96
Gómez Millas, Juan, 93
González, Eugenio, 93
Grove, Marmaduque, 88
Guaicaipuro, 31
Guzmán Blanco, Antonio, 18–19, 25, 69,
    81

Hahn, Jurgen, 45, 134n29
Hegel, 63, 65
Henríque Ureña, Pedro, 20, 23, 127
Himno del desterrado (Heredia), 24
*Historia de la literatura venezolana en el
    siglo diez y nueve* (Picón Febres),
    29–32
Historia de la poesía hispanoamericana
    (Menéndez y Pelayo), 29
Hitler, 106
Hubner, Sara, 92
Hus, Jan 109
Hombre y la historia (Fortoul), 28

Ibañez, Carlos, 88, 90
incultura (lack of culture), meaning of,
    112; *See also* Picón Salas
Indice, 93–94
*Indice crítico de la literatura lati-
    noamericana* (Zum Felde), 34
Infortunios de Alonso Ramírez (Sigüen-
    za y Góngora), 24
inteligencia venezolana (Venezuelan in-
    telligence), meaning of, 53, 58; *See
    also* Picón Salas
Irazábal, Carlos, 18 131n3

Kant, 86
Keyserling, 106
Korn, Guillermo, 26

Lazarillo de ciegos caminantes (Carrió
    de la Vendera), 24
Letras, 93
López Contreras, Eleazar, 94, 98

Machado, Antonio, 27
Mallarmé, 39
Mariano Picón Salas (Siso Martínez), 64
Mariátegui, José Carlos, 20–21
Maricastaña, 121–22, 139n9

Mármol, Luis Enrique, 27
Martí, 82
Martínez, José Luis, 34
Marx, 63, 84
Masaryk, Thomas, 109
Massiani, Felipe, 28
Medina, José Ramón, 25, 27
Mérida, 61, 123–26; *See also* Picón Salas
Mijares, Augusto, 65
Miliani, Domingo, 30
Miranda, Francisco de, 43, 95, 128
Mistral, Gabriela, 40
Monagas, José Tadeo, 19, 25, 69, 96
Montaigne, 34
Mosáico de política y literatura (López
    Méndez), 32

Neruda, Pablo, 92–93
Newton, Isaac, 37
Nueva historia de literatura americana
    (Sánchez), 30
Nuevos poetas venezolanos (Olivares
    Figueroa), 32

Oropesa, Juan, 28
Ortega y Gasset, José, 20

Paéz, José Antonio, 19, 58, 96
Paramaconi, 31
Parnaso venezolano (Calcaño), 32
patria, meaning of, 57, 59, 112, 129; as
    patria chica, 61; as patria entrañable,
    79; as patria geográfica, 79; as patria
    grande, 60; *See also* Picón Salas
Paz Castillo, 27
Perquillo Sarniento, El (Fernández de
    Lizardi), 24
Perón, Juan, 106
pícaro, 24, 49, 70; *See also* Picón Salas
Picón Febres, Gonzalo, 25
Picón Salas, Mariano (1901–1965), a
    universal man of letters, 23; an intel-
    lectual awakening, 67–71; in Caracas,
    75–78; in Chile, 78–94; on Cain and
    Abel, 71; on cultura (culture), 101,
    112, 115; on Czechoslovakia, 109; on
    democracy, 110, on devenir (becom-
    ing), 62–76, on errancia (peregrina-
    tion), 24, 44–51; on France, 104–105;
    on Germany, 105–106; on intellectual

freedom, 88; on Italy, 106–107; on love and compassion, 84–87–88, on Marxism, 90–92; on Mérida, 47, 51, 61, 123–26; on Pablo Neruda, 92–93; on political idealogies, 98; on Spain, 107–108; on the concept of *el disimulo*, 80–81; on the essay, 35–40; on the function of the artist and teacher, 83; on the intellectual and Don Quixote, 86; on the meaning of *patria*, 58–61; on the moral obligations of men of letters, 33; on the *pícaro*, 70; on the United States, 109–11; on Venezuela, 111–17; on the Venezuelan exodus of 1923, 77–78; on Venezuelan literary criticism, 30–31; search for authenticity, 40–42, 54–61; search for identity, 48; travels of, 22–23

WORKS:

"Año 1920, El", 70

"Amor, en fin que todo diga y cante," 84

Buscando el camino, 47–51, 54–61, 70, 118, 125

Comprensión de Venezuela, 62, 111–17

De la conquista a la independencia, 46

Europa-América, preguntas a la esfinge de la cultura, 23, 101–11

Hispano-américa, una posición crítica, 46

Malos salvajes, Los, 46, 60, 65

Mundo imaginario, 51, 54–55, 60, 67–73, 95

Obras selectas, 54

Odlsea de tierra firme, 41, 61, 68

Registro de huéspedes, 92, 97

Regreso de tres mundos, 43, 75

Tratos de la noche, Los, 46

Plato, 26

Portales, Diego, 80

positivism, authentic, 26; scientific, 19, 25–28

Problema de América, El (Mayz Vallenilla), 51

Prometheus, 91

Revista Nacional de Cultura, 94

Reyes, Alfonso, 20–23, 34, 53, 127

Reyes, Salvador, 93

Ripoll, Carlos, 34

Robespierre, 85

Rodó, José Enrique, 20–21, 110, 131n7

Roosevelt, Franklin D., 110

Rosas, Juan Manuel, 19, 81

Rosenblat, Angel, 24

Royal-Dutch-Shell Corporation, 73

Savanarola, 85

Sarmiento, Domingo Faustino, 20–21, 24, 36

Siete ensayos en busca de la realidad peruana (Mariátegui), 21

Silva Castro, Raul, 93

Sorocaima, 31

Spain, 107–108

Tamanaco, 31

tierra, meaning of, 112; *See also* Picón Salas

Toro Fermín, 25

tradición dinámica, meaning of, 120

tradición estática, meaning of, 120

Tuina, 31

Ultima Tule (Reyes), 53

Ulysses, 91

Unamuno, 36, 53

United States, 109–11; economic and political hegemony, 19

Uslar Pietri, Arturo, 23, 28, 95

Vallenilla Lanz, Laureano, 57, 131n2

Vasconcelos, José, 20–21, 64, 127

Venezuela, 111–17; errancia venezolano (Venezuelan peregrination), 24; venezolanidad, significance of, 40, 53, 112, 124, 128-29; Venezuelan culture, 42; Venezuelan exodus of 1923, 77–78; Wars of Federation, 17; *See also* Picón Salas

Venezuelan Prose Fiction (Ratcliff), 29

Viajes por Europa, Africa, América (Sarmiento), 21

Viallavicencia, Rafael, 26–27

Voltaire, 36

Wise, George S., 18

Zumeta, César, 28

Zum Felde, 34